GOLDFIELDS STORIES

Early Days in Western Australia

Volume One

LORRAINE KELLY & NORMA KING

Illustrations by Lorraine Kelly

Goldfields Stories: Early Days in Western Australia

Copyright © 2018 by Lorraine Kelly.

All rights reserved.

No part of this book may be used or reproduced in any manner whatsoever without written permission except in the case of brief quotations embodied in critical articles or reviews.

For information contact:

Lorraine Kelly
27 Valentine Way, Australind WA 6233

goldfieldstories.com
@goldfieldstories

Book and Cover design by Lorraine Kelly - LozsArt

ISBN: 978-0-9876322-2-7

First Edition: December 2018

Acknowledgments

I would like to thank my family for allowing me to archive and use Norma King's research. It is an honour to have at my disposal her life time's work. I would also like to thank everyone who has encouraged me to write and self-publish this book.

My Nanna's book, 'Colourful Tales of the Western Australian Goldfields' was the inspiration for this book. I have revised, researched, and illustrated some of the stories it contained. As such, even though Norma is no longer with us, it is a book co-authored between us.

In the acknowledgments to her book, she thanked:

- Hocking and Co. and West Australian Newspapers Ltd for allowing her to reproduce articles she wrote for their publications;
- the Eastern Goldfields branch of the Western Australian Historical Society for providing material for use in the book;
- her brother-in-law Bernie Rutland for the idea of the book;
- Baron Hill for permission to include his poem "End of the Rainbow";
- her daughter Zena and husband Howard for their advice and criticism; and
- the many people who told their stories and provided photos.

I trust you will enjoy these stories as much as I did in researching them.

Contents

Acknowledgments	i
Financial conversion	i
Authors' Note	i
Death Is Nothing at All	iii
Norma King	iv
Lorraine Kelly	v
Pocket Hercules - Dinny O'Callaghan	1
McCann's Duffer Rush	24
When Kanowna was Young	41
The Wail of a Dryblower	68
Darlot: A Rush in the Wilderness	71
Darlot (for Dad)	87
The Cycle Specials of Coolgardie	88
The Not-So-Modest Smiler Hales	101
'Roll-up': The Law of the Diggers	112
1897 Tragedy Cost Six Lives	119
Her Final Walk	125
The Happy Loopline Train	131

The Fabulous Londonderry	141
Wealth of Nations and Dunnsville	151
Tom Dimer: Son of a Pioneer	161
Merton and Mertondale	172
When Nobody Cared	191
People Mentioned	195
Works Cited	200

Financial Conversion

To help translate the value of the pound in today's term, the 1890's average wage was £150 per annum. They needed to produce thirty ounces of gold a year to make an average salary (Compton).

Authors' Note

This book contains many quotes that are now culturally unacceptable. They are included as it represents the use of the language used in early Australia. This language does not express the authors' opinions.

Although this book is based on 'Colourful Tales of the Western Australian Goldfields', it is somewhat different. This is particularly so for the account of Merton and his find. A thesis by Chappell examined the myths surrounding him and the operation of the mine in detail. It would have been remiss of me to continue the myths which are no longer supported by facts she uncovered. I found her thesis very interesting and am indebted for her insight and vigorous study.

The Tom Dimer story was not in the original book. This story has come from her research and interviews she taped with him in the 1970's and 1980's. I have restored and published these interviews. You can find them at Goldfieldstories.com.

The poem "Death is Nothing at All" was written by Henry Scott-

Holland (1847-1918). He was a priest at St. Paul's Cathedral of London. It was part of a sermon he gave while the body of King Edward VII was lying in state at Westminster. It was also read at my Nanna's funeral, and I feel as though she is in the next room now.

Death Is Nothing at All

By Henry Scott-Holland

Death is nothing at all.
It does not count.
I have only slipped away into the next room.
Nothing has happened.

Everything remains exactly as it was.
I am I, and you are you,
and the old life that we lived so fondly together is untouched, unchanged.
Whatever we were to each other, that we are still.

Call me by the old familiar name.
Speak of me in the easy way which you always used.
Put no difference into your tone.
Wear no forced air of solemnity or sorrow.

Laugh as we always laughed at the little jokes that we enjoyed together.
Play, smile, think of me, pray for me.
Let my name be ever the household word that it always was.
Let it be spoken without an effort, without the ghost of a shadow upon it.

Life means all that it ever meant.
It is the same as it ever was.
There is absolute and unbroken continuity.
What is this death but a negligible accident?

Why should I be out of mind because I am out of sight?
I am but waiting for you, for an interval,
somewhere very near,
just around the corner.

All is well.
Nothing is hurt; nothing is lost.
One brief moment and all will be as it was before.
How we shall laugh at the trouble of parting when we meet again!

NORMA KING
1922-2014

Norma was born in Kalgoorlie in 1922. A life member of the Eastern Goldfields Historical Society, she spent her life living and recording history in the region. Her work on social history was particularly important, documenting where people in the Goldfields came from, where they stayed and what they achieved.

In 1972 she published her first book, "Nickel Country, Gold Country". Seven more books followed, being: Colourful Tales of the Western Australian Goldfields (1980), The Waldeck Story (1980), Daughters of Midas (1988), Wings Over the Goldfields (1992), The Voice of the Goldfields (1995), The Hannans Club – The first 100 Years (1996), and her autobiography, "Then They Called me Norma" (2003). She also wrote numerous historical pamphlets and articles for the *Kalgoorlie Miner*.

She was also a life member of the WA section of the Fellowship of Australian Writers and The Golden Mile Art Group. In 2013, she received the OAM (Order of Australia) for her service to the Community as a Historian. In 2014 she was included in Kalgoorlie's walk of fame in Hannan Street.

Lorraine Kelly

Lorraine is Norma's Grand-daughter. Born in Kalgoorlie, Lorraine moved to Perth with her family at ten years of age. After completing a Bachelor of Arts Degree in English and History at UWA, she worked in the Finance Industry in Perth. In 1997 she moved to Australind to raise her family.

From 2017-2018 she created and self-published several adult colouring books. In 2018 she also began archiving Norma King's research material. This resulted in the publication of this book. The cover design, interior, illustrations were done by Lorraine, under the name of LozsArt.

For more information regarding this book, go to goldfieldstories.com.

Chapter One

Pocket Hercules - Dinny O'Callaghan

WHEN COOLGARDIE WAS NEW and luring men from all parts of the country, many interesting characters rode or trudged into town. Among them was pint-sized, bantam-weight Dennis (Dinny) O'Callaghan, who was also known as "Pocket Hercules".

Dinny arrived from Broken Hill on 4 February 1893, eleven days before his eighteenth birthday. With just over three pounds in his pocket he was 1,500 miles from his parents' home; "too far away to go home for a good dinner or a good bed at night." He left behind his family that had immigrated from Ireland, and he did not know a soul in his new town.

He was already an experienced digger as he had been working in the goldfields in South Australia from age ten. When the government officials made their periodic raids on miners to check mining rights, they allowed him to continue mining even though he was too young to hold a licence.

Upon arrival at Coolgardie, he immediately set up his 6x8 foot tent. Within hours he was fossicking for gold. He got a few shillings worth on his first day.

It was a dusty town due to the dryblowing activities of the prospectors, and the buildings were mostly canvas. There were three-hundred men on the field, and as he expected, it looked a poor place to live. The population of Coolgardie in the early days was made up of men from all parts of the globe. Quite a lot had previous mining or business experience from Ballarat, Bendigo in Victoria, New South Wales, New Zealand, America, Mt. Brown, Tetulpa, and Broken Hill.

The best of the alluvial gold had been taken, but he managed to get some gold at Fly Shoot Flat and Hogan Gully. As most of the men went over the ground quickly with a sieve within a week, there was still a lot of fine gold. He did well here for about three months by treating the soil another four inches deeper with dry blowing dishes.

In those days, if you left your claim for a rush or any other reason, nothing would be taken. He would leave a pick or a shovel on the claim to denote his intentions of returning to it. If anyone did get caught stealing, there would be a 'roll-up', and if found guilty they would be given a few days to vacate the fields.

After three months he decided to prospect farther afield. He bought pack horses and ventured out into the unknown country. He rode on one horse with a swag tied in front of him on the saddle. By the time he put tools and water on the other horse, he could only take enough food for six weeks.

After nearly perishing on one expedition due to lack of water, he sold his tough little Brumbies with the idea of purchasing camels for his future expeditions.

Dinny then tried his luck at White Feather (Kanowna) but always seemed to be drawn back to Coolgardie, as "those days in Coolgardie were wild and willing and it was where I spent some of the happiest days of my life."

After selling a gold lease in Coolgardie for two-hundred pounds, he went to Kalgoorlie and got some gold on a small claim at the foot of Maritana Hill. After working it out, he was yet again drawn back to Coolgardie.

He soon decided to go on another expedition with a friend named George to explore the Lake Way district, which is around four-hundred miles north of Coolgardie. They couldn't afford camels, so he travelled with horses again. The region at this time had places where "white man had never put a foot on".

They had to keep watch for hostile Aboriginals and often saw their fresh foot tracks. They always kept their guns loaded and woke well before daylight, as this was when attacks were more prevalent. At Cosmanouve Hills they found a little sandy, gravel creek of fresh water. They camped there, taking turns keeping guard at night. The horses were restless, indicating they could smell or hear Aboriginals.

In the morning, two young, naked Aboriginal teenage girls hesitantly approached them. They appeared frightened, and Dinny was concerned they were sent by their leader to trap them. He warned his mate to have nothing to do with them if he cared for their lives. His mate was losing control of himself and wanted to make up with one of them. Dinny had to remind him again that it could be a trap. They gave the girls some salted meat with damper and then sent them away. Unsure of the tribe's intentions, they quickly filled their water drums and left. His mate was a bit sulky with Dinny for a few days but eventually returned to his usual fair temperament.

Two nights later they were camped by a waterhole. As it looked like rain, they had pitched a tent. They were standing in the tent with a candle, preparing for bed when spears came through the tent. Fortunately, the spears missed them by about six inches. Dinny quickly kicked over the candle, grabbed his rifle and fired a shot in the air to scare them off. They then took turns keeping watch for the rest of the night. The attackers did not return. Dinny believed they must have left the area that night travelling with firesticks. His mate now believed him that the girls were a trap, as they thought the attack came from the same tribe.

They prospected around that area for three days without success. They took their time returning to Coolgardie. For food, they shot Kangaroos, emus, turkeys, and wild birds. They carried salt to preserve the meat, but the "game was very scarce; likewise the gold". The whole journey took around three months.

Dinny did not divulge the full name of his mate in his book as he did not want George's children to find out about his "naughty desires when a young man". George later worked on one of the big steamships, and they met again on one of Dinny's many travels. Dinny wrote: "He was a real good mate in the bush. I often chaffed him on the steamer about him getting the sulks with me. He enjoyed the reminder".

In early 1894, news spread around Coolgardie about a gold rush that was around nineteen miles north-west of Kalgoorlie. Teamsters were charging to take men's swags out to the spot. Dinny and three mates left Coolgardie together with their swags aboard a teamster. It took them two days to get to the Wild Cat Rush, as it turned out to be. Most of the men returned with the teamsters as no one was getting gold and there was no water. Despite this, Dinny and his party decided to stay for a few days.

The teamster could only sell them a couple of gallons of water. They decided that two of them would travel to Kalgoorlie to get water and Dinny would stay behind to do some dryblowing. They used a gallon of water by the next morning and then halved the remaining water. His mates went on their way with half the water, leaving him with half a gallon.

Dinny worked hard dryblowing all morning without a drink. By lunchtime he was very thirsty, so he placed his billy directly on the fire so the water would boil quickly. The fire shifted, and all his water was spilled. He was so annoyed that he put the toe plate of his hobnail blucher boot through the bottom of his billy.

After dryblowing all afternoon, he was hungry and thirsty. As he had no water or food, he had a difficult night's sleep. The next day he just sat in the shade waiting for his mates to return. They were walking, so they did not return until after sunset the next day. Dinny said that hard times like these "… makes one hardy and able to appreciate good times when he gets them".

They all concluded that it was a duffer rush and they should leave. Fortunately, some men came into their camp that night, and they returned with them to Coolgardie.

Dinny's luck improved with the discovery of the fabulous 'Hole of Gold' at Londonderry, nineteen kilometres south of Coolgardie. He was camped on Bailey Street near George Bailey's condensers when George told him he was heading out to peg a lease at a phenomenally rich discovery. He said he would peg a lease for him too provided he sell his water and keep the find secret. Dinny agreed.

When news of the find spread, about two-hundred diggers swarmed to the spot and pegged claims surrounding the mine. Dinny sold out for £1,000. He then looked around for more ground to peg but found that it had all been taken. He then had a brainwave.

In those days, an alluvial gold miner could work to within six metres of the cap of a reef (later this was changed to fifteen metres) provided that the lease was then only recommended for approval. The owner of the lease had all rights to reefs or lodes. The owners of Londonderry had their line of reefs delineated with red flags. The Mining Act did not allow them to hold alluvial ground where their tents and log hut were situated. Dinny's bright idea was to peg an alluvial claim on this ground.

Their log hut held the precious specimen stones from the mine. At night there was a man on watch with a revolver. The guard would sometimes fire a shot or two to let people know he was there. That log hut was sometimes like a jeweller's shop or a gold mint with gold specimens. 'Big Ben' was a beauty, it took four men to lift it.

After the log hut was their six tents. They were further away in a row. There was sound alluvial ground on a road in front of their tents that the trade cart used. Dinny started to peg a block of fifty feet square, which held the tents and the famous log hut.

Jim Shaw, the first mayor of Coolgardie and manager of the Londonderry, was very annoyed when he saw what Dinny was doing, as were the six shareholders. They told him they couldn't put up with it, but Dinny replied "you will have to put up with it. Go and read the Mining Act".

Poor young Peter Carter, the youngest shareholder said, "You can't peg in our fireplace". Dinny retorted, "The last time I read the Mining Act I did not read anything about your fireplace in it." and nearly all the men roared with laughter.

While he was pegging, a lot of the men had their eyes and mouths wide open. One of the prospectors said that he was not allowed to peg in their tents. Dinny replied that if you had six big tents like the circuses have, you could cover nearly all the alluvial ground near the reef where the gold is, then no one would have any ground. Dinny said they were getting plenty of gold and they should not begrudge him getting a bit.

John Mills went to see to Warden Finnerty, but he was soon told that Dinny was within his rights. After working his new claim for only five days, Dinny heard of another rich find a few kilometres away. This find was 'The Wealth of Nations'. Dinny came to a suitable arrangement with the prospectors, so he sold it to them. They re-pegged his lease and took it over.

Before leaving, Carter invited him to share a large bottle of champagne at the Club Hotel. Dinny said he "did not look too flash in my old bush clothes and billycan and bag in hand - and me drinking champagne in a hotel with a man of fame!"

Dinny and Carter shared a few bottles of champagne together. Carter walked with him until they caught up with the camel team he was to travel with. Carter asked why he didn't get a horse, spring cart and six months tucker and look for a good show. Dinny replied that it takes a lot of money to go exploring for gold. Carter then offered to lend him the money in future if he had no luck in this rush. Dinny thought this was good of him because they had only recently met. It seems Carter forgave him for pegging their fireplace!

Dinny was on the first camel team to the rush. Luck was on his side as he found 450 ounces in nine days. One nugget was sent to his father in a mustard tin as a gift. He also gave two-hundred ounces to Lord John Forrest to put in the bank for him when he got to Coolgardie, which he did. When the gold around the new find became scarce, he charged his revolver, rolled up his swag and set off down a lonely track to walk the thirty-seven miles back to Coolgardie.

On the way, he slept in a shed at a store. He covered himself with a tarpaulin so he couldn't be easily seen. Dinny was unaware that two men he had been warned about had followed him from the Wealth of Nations. They came into the shed looking for him. He could hear them whispering so he put his hand on his revolver in case they lifted the tarpaulin. Fortunately, they left the shed. They made a noise while looking for him around the store. The boss of the store shouted out "who's there?" They then ran off, he had yet another lucky escape.

By mid-1894 when Dinny was not quite twenty, Coolgardie had ample supplies of hotels, grocery shops, butcher shops, bakers, drapers, greengrocers, a chemist, soft drinks, hard drinks, shanties, and brothels with French or Japanese women. Dinny decided that the busy centre needed a smallgoods shop that sold fresh oysters, crayfish, ham and eggs. He opened the York Ham Shop with his partner Billy Reynolds.

They sold all types of smallgoods, but the biggest drawcard was oysters at five shillings a dozen. The oysters and crayfish came from Perth by mail coach from the head of the railway line, which was at Doodlakine at that point. The coach would have travelled over three-hundred kilometres from the railway station to Coolgardie.

On opening night, he displayed his gold nuggets in the shop window as a drawcard to get people to look at his display of eatables.

They made a roaring trade as they got in first-class goods. The hotels and boarding houses were good customers. Fried eggs and ham was a favourite, and they sold hundreds of dozens of oysters per week in their shells. If anyone bought a few dozen oysters, they got a complimentary oyster opener.

One night four men came in and had an eating contest between themselves. The person who ate the least had to pay the bill. The person who ate the most was a little, very dark Frenchman, "not tall enough to cut a cabbage from its roots". He ate thirty-two eggs and about one pound of the best English ham. The loser quite happily paid the five-pound bill.

A good yarn about this oyster bar got circulated in the newspapers

Pocket Hercules - Dinny O'Callaghan

from a piece written by the columnist called "Dryblower". (*Sunday Times* [Perth], 12 November 1916). Dryblower claimed Dinny told him the story. However, Dinny did not write about it in his book and an article in the *Sunday Times* on 7 June 1925, claimed it did not happen. An article in 1921 does claim that Dinny's first batch of oysters ran out quickly, so he got the tinned variety and used the shells over and over. Maybe there is some truth in the story, or perhaps it was Dryblower's imaginings that were often repeated, we shall never know for sure! (*Sunday Times* [Perth], 19 June 1921 p14)

Anyway, the story was that the coach driver carting his oysters decided they had been dead too long, so he threw them off his coach about forty kilometres away from Coolgardie. Not wanting his oysters to be totally wasted, Dinny had a brainwave. He collected his oysters in a light cart and then emptied and washed the shells. He bought all the tinned oysters available and ordered more from Perth. When customers ordered his 'fresh' oysters, he would put the tinned oyster in the shells. After their meal, the shells would be washed for the next order. This went on for some time, the shells gradually disappearing through 'breakage, riot and old age', until only eighteen were left.

One night a teamster from York, who had never seen oysters, came to the shop and ordered steak and eggs, but was told it was off the menu. The sign advertising oysters caught his eye, so he decided to try them. A few minutes later Dinny heard a loud grating noise, almost like a quartz grinding machine. He rushed from the back of the shop towards where the sound was coming from. "The skins of these 'ere things is very tough", growled the teamster, pointing to a ground-up mass on the table. He had chewed up the shells, thus ending Dinny's fresh oyster scam.

In any event, whether Dinny sold fresh oysters or tinned, he got tired of being tied to the shop "like a dog to a wagon", so they decided to sell it, and he began prospecting again.

Sometime in 1985, Dinny was on his fourth expedition with a greenhorn Englishman named Joe Morton. Morton wanted colonial experiences, which he certainly got with Dinny. They had thirsty travels on camels, were early arrivals at Lake Darlot and worked an alluvial claim on the south end of David Carnegie's (*Daily News*, [Perth], 25 August 1934, p19).

Dinny had an experience with a mad camel near Dingo Creek. He was travelling on a single bush track on his camel when a big, active bull on season came rushing at him. Fortunately, it was hobbled. Dinny let it pass, but it decided it wanted to cause them trouble. Dinny's camel was not usually a fast mover, but it was as scared as Dinny and ran very fast on this occasion. The mad camel was jumping in its hobbles. Apparently, a camel can travel very quickly when jumping, but it must stop to rest after a few hundred yards to recuperate.

The mad camel got within about twenty-five yards of them on five or six occasions. Dinny decided that if the camel caught up to them, he would jump off his camel and make for a tree. He also kept his eye open for a long stick with which to defend himself. He knew that if the camel caught up to them while he was still riding, it could pull him off and kill him. Fortunately, the camel finally gave up the chase.

When Dinny got to the Ninety Mile townsite, a man and an Afghan cameleer asked him if he had seen a mad camel on the track. They told him that this camel had an Afghan up a tree for eight hours. They put one bullet in its neck and another in its belly before it ran off. The camel belonged to a man named Jim Kay and Kay had lost his arm due to a bite the camel had previously given him. Dinny knew Jim Kay and the camel. The camel could carry a half ton all day when bulling.

Camels were important in the goldfields for moving freight and exploring arid areas. The advantages of camels in the goldfields at this time was well explained by George Robertson and Company in his pamphlet called *'The Coolgardie Goldfields'*, published in 1895:

> The only animal fit to travel with or to work, and by far the most economical is the camel. Suppose, for example, you desire to send out food, tools, explosives, and water to a camp, say 50 miles from Coolgardie. If you were to send these stores by horse teams, you must also load up your wagon with feed and water for your horses on the outward and return journey. Camels are watered before they start, and there is splendid feed for them in the bush in almost every direction you like to travel, and when you return to town in four or five days' time, you then re-water the camels at the original starting point. Feed for your camels is not purchased, and water is required only at the cheapest depot once in five or six days. ... The camels are coming surely enough - from Bourke, from Adelaide, from India, and from Afghanistan, in hundreds. They have already located themselves in this great, dry goldfields district by thousands, and they are a fixture. This is the future home of the camel and of the bicycle. A bicycle requires no water nor any feed except a little oil, and 10 miles an hour is very frequently accomplished on most of the tracks where a pair of horses in a buckboard on an outward journey, loaded up with horse feed and water, will only cover at the most 6 miles, with the

roads as they are now. The bicycle, it will thus be seen, has also come to stay as a rapid and economical means of locomotion at Coolgardie.

Dinny excelled at boxing and liked to spar with fighters in the gyms. He claimed he was never the cause of any fights or got it into his head that he could fight. He said he thought himself lucky if he won. Despite this, there seem to be quite a few reports of his fighting prowess and him getting into fights.

The first fight he had in Coolgardie was in 1894 at the Reynolds Hotel. He got into 'holts' with a large young man who was in the company of five other men. All these men were over six foot and looked like brothers. The young man was using bad language to one of the barmaids, so Dinny 'spoke to him about it'. The man tried to hit him but missed. Dinny didn't, so they all started fighting Dinny. He was receiving punches from all directions and Dinny was spreading his punches evenly between them. They could not knock him down.

Jack Kiernan and his friends came to his aid and stopped them. Jack called them a lot of damned curs, pulled a roll of notes out of his pockets and said he would back Dinny to beat all six of them, one after another. They decided against this and quickly left the bar. Dinny never saw them again.

He claims his hardest fight was with Billie Williams in Coolgardie in 1897. Draughts was a popular pastime, and if there was a wager on a game a large crowd would soon gather. Mr Brown was considered the best player in the fields at that time. (He was an agent for Wilkie Bros. who built the line from Northam to Coolgardie goldfields.) He was offering to give any man on the fields a draw-start for a wager. This meant he would count a draw as a win to his opponent. Dinny took up the challenge, and a fifty-pound wager was set. On the day, more than a hundred miners gathered to watch and bet.

Dinny concentrated solely on getting draws and won three draws in a row, which was a great feat against the champion. He was betting on himself and had won three-hundred pounds so far. Heavy-weight boxing champion of Western Australia, Billy Williams like Dinny's style, so he started backing him.

Much to Mr Brown's annoyance, he won two more games by drawing. A friend of Mr Brown's kept whispering in his ear. He was advising him not to give the draw, as Dinny was too good. Dinny was getting annoyed at the hanger-on-friend not minding his own business.

The sixth game looked as though Brown would win, but Dinny set a trap and managed to win another draw. When he fell into the trap, Brown admitted he was beaten, but Brown's friend poked his nose in again and said, "If Mr Brown took three kings the other way, it would not be a draw".

Dinny saw this as an opportunity to make Brown's friend look foolish in front of about one-hundred spectators, so he said, "I will show you that you do not know what you are talking about". Billy Williams objected and growled at Dinny: "You're not going to show them any of your tricks". Billy was winning a lot of money, so he didn't want to start losing now.

Dinny started to put the twelve kings on the board to show them, but Billy pushed them off the board. Dinny told him that it had nothing to do with him and exclaimed; "What right have you to dictate to me;

you are not my father". When he started to put the kings on the board again, Billy hit him on the nose. Of course, this upset Dinny. He thought it was a cowardly act to hit him without warning.

Reproduction of an image in "Wigs Upon the Green" *Western Mail*, [Perth], 22 April 1954, p10

Pocket Hercules - Dinny O'Callaghan

The heavyweight weighed 14 ½ stone, Dinny only 8 ½. Dinny thought this was a reasonable match so hopped into him. Billy got into such a temper he started frothing at the mouth "like a bull camel on season". The crowd was afraid to try and stop him, and they told Dinny to run away. He said, "Never in your life", and kept on mixing it pretty well with Billy.

He threw Dinny and fell on him with full weight. Spasms of pain ran right through him like an electric shock. Billy began hitting Dinny wildly, so the crowd pulled him off him. Dinny was now as mad as ever and hoed back into him. Billy was out of condition, so he sat down for thirty seconds. Dinny pranced around him saying he was a big coward, who was not satisfied at being six stone heavier and hit him when he was down. That roused Billy up again out of his seat. Dinny shot in and hit him on the nose. Billy charged at him in pain, but Dinny took him in a wrestling hold and tossed him in the air. Billy damaged an elbow and a knee when he hit the ground. They were hard at it when a five-foot-eleven bank clerk who was good with his hands decided to intervene on Dinny's behalf. Billy turned on the clerk. Grasping the chance, Dinny locked the heavy-weights arms.

Now almost berserk, Billy sank his teeth into Dinny's arm. At this point, the crowd moved in and successfully pulled them apart. Dinny didn't want to stop. It took a group of them to carry him away by the arms and legs. His 'rescuers' locked him in a pantry of the hotel. One of his friends stayed with him until he calmed down. His friend then escorted him to his room and Dinny was finally content to rest. Dinny started to feel dreadful. Vowing he would never fight again, he rang the bell for some well-needed whiskies, which greatly helped his recovery. While resting, the events that led up to the fight kept going over in his mind. As they were both winning a lot of money before their brawl, he got angry at Billy all over again. Dinny was to be married soon, and he wanted the money to buy his wife-to-be a nice gift.

Giving up his resolution not to fight again he jumped out of bed in a crazed state. After rushing down the stairs, he saw Billy at the bar and ran towards him, determined to take off more skin. Poor Billy put out his hand for Dinny to take, embraced him and started to cry. He said, "I fought my little mate" and tears ran down his face as big as pigeon's eggs. He then shouted: "Champaign for all!" Dinny later claimed he was a good mate, but a bit hot-tempered at times like himself.

Dinny was soon after married by Father Long. It was the third marriage to occur in Coolgardie. The church was a tent and a bough shed. He claimed his son was the first white boy to be born in Boulder. He also laid claim to being the first to peg in the famous 'Sacred Nugget' or 'Golden Sickle' rush at Kanowna. This was perhaps the most sensational and exciting goldrush to take place in Western Australia.

This rush took place in 1898. Father Long, who was mentioned above, told a friend that some men had shown him a slug of gold weighing about forty-five kilograms. He had been sworn to secrecy and vowed not to reveal the names of the men concerned. They told him he could disclose the locality of the find in three weeks' time.

His friend must have told others, as the news spread throughout Australia and even as far as New Zealand. During those weeks Father

Long was constantly pestered for information. On 11 August at 2pm, he appeared on a hotel balcony at Kanowna and addressed the thousands of men waiting in the street. He told them that the nugget had been found on the south side of Mount Glynn, eleven kilometres along the Kurnalpi road. A poem was later published about the incident ("Rhyme and Reason" *Melbourne Punch*, 18 August 1898, p6):

> No clergyman had ever had a more attentive flock,
> The people came from all directions crushing,
> They waited for the preacher with one eye upon the clock,
> All ready when the signal came for rushing.
>
> The father told them tersely of the troubles that he bore.
> 'Gainst callers grim to make a stern resistance.
> Then made the statement, and remarked he wished to say some more,
> But, whoop! The crowd was fading in the distance.
>
> The cleric stood all desolate within an empty waste,
> And looked about in wondering dejection.
> Then he cried with all his might,
> "There ain't no reason in this haste, Come back!
> Ye've disremembered the collection!

Dinny was on the outskirts of the crowd with a saddled horse and got away quickly. Tassie O'Connor and a mounted trooper were not far behind him.

Arriving at the place described, Dinny saw a few freshly dug, shallow holes, so he jumped off his horse and began pegging. The other two men were close behind and hammered in their pegs nearby. The rest of the crowd arrived and pegged whatever they could. However, by the time Dinny had pegged his claim, he said he would have sold out cheaply as he did not like the look of the ground at all. Neither did a lot of other men: many did not even bother to put a peg in the field.

The men soon realised that the story of the nugget was only a practical joke played on the Father. If the perpetrators of the hoax had been discovered, they would probably have been lynched.

It was estimated that the rush cost the public £40,000 (*Western Mail*, [Perth],16 December 1898, p123). It was rumoured that some of the town's businessmen may have been responsible. This was because a government inspection party was visiting Kanowna to decide what extra services the town required. A rush at this time would have highlighted the need for more services.

Father Long took the names of those who had misled him to his grave. Unfortunately, this wasn't long as he died of typhoid less than a year later (Bough).

In 1912, Dinny moved to Perth. For some years he was the champion pigeon shot of the state and was also prominent with the rifle. It was at this time he also began his most successful business venture. Motor cars were taking over from horses and buggies. He purchased a car and worked as a taxi driver and had plenty of time to think while waiting for fares. He decided to invent something that would make him rich. He came up with a simple idea that made him £10,000 in two years and enabled him to travel the world twice.

At this time, petrol was tipped into the tanks of motor cars from cans. It was difficult to do this without spilling the fuel. Dinny invented a gadget to put on petrol tins for easier pouring. He patented it the

"O'Callaghan Ezyfiller". It sold well throughout Australia and New Zealand.

On 1 March 1917 at 9.15pm, Dinny was charged for using insulting language to a Constable Callaghan. The reports in the paper highlight his infamous Irish temperament.

Constable Callaghan and a few other constables approached a large crowd outside the Strand Café in Hay Street Perth as they were causing a traffic jam. In the middle of the group were Dinny and his car. Constable Callaghan asked him to move it, but Dinny refused, stating he was looking after it. Dinny told Callaghan: "I don't care a ---- for the police; there are some good constables and there are some ---- mongrels, and you are one". He drove the car away but returned and called out "Good night, Callaghan". Dinny was slightly under the influence of drink.

Dinny had previously tried to sue Constable Callaghan for a one-pound fare but lost the case. Due to their history, Dinny obviously enjoyed heckling the constable in the street and later at court.

At Court Dinny's lawyer, Mr Harney, asked the constable if he went to the war under an assumed name. The constable replied that it had nothing to do with the case, but Harney persisted and asked what name he enlisted with.

Callaghan replied "I will make an explanation if you think it will do you any good. At the outbreak of the war, I was a constable in the Western Australian police force and was a deserter from the Imperial Army. For that reason, I went away under an assumed name."

The prosecutor, Sergeant Lean, said "That is the whole secret, I hope you are satisfied".

Mr Harney then asked Callaghan if he had a temper to which he replied he had a "fairly soft temper". There was some laughter in the court. Harney then asked, "Don't you think it was reasonable for the defendant to be on the footpath looking after his car when there was a crowd about?" Callaghan replied that Dinny was looking for a fight.

A witness said he was surprised that the constable allowed Dinny to use such language in the streets and that the police were not excited about it.

Harney asked Callaghan if there was old enmity between him and Dinny. He replied, "Certainly not. Well, you came here to put this 'pot' on. I came here as a citizen of Perth to put a stop to the language of this kind being used in the streets."

Dinny then took the stand and said that when he drove up to the Strand Café, he could see there was going to be a row. There was a crowd on the footpath around an Afghan, and until they went away, he could not leave his car. He said the constable approached him in a bombastic way and Dinny said, "I am sorry to say that our names are nearly the same; mine is Dinny, and I am proud of it; there are a lot of people in this world who drop the 'O' in their names, because they think they would get on better." He then said that he would be silly to use such language in front of so many constables but admitted to saying that there are some good men in the force and some mongrels.

The prosecutor then said, "You say some disparaging things about the constable, and then point to the fact that he went to the war under an assumed name. Have you been to the war yourself?" to which Dinny replied, "No, but I think I could have done as much as he did". To which Sergeant Lean retorted "Never mind that! You were not there to see anyway".

Another witness, Henry Lowry stated that the crowd was so thick, Dinny could not wind up his car and that Dinny said to Callaghan "I would like to get you in my car: big as you are, I would throw you out".

Another witness called Charles Pearson advised the court that he often narrated "Dinny's oration in Hay Street" to his friends because of O'Callaghan's calmness at the time he spoke to the police.

Sergeant Lean then asked, "You must have admired the oration to take that much notice of it" to which he replied, "I did admire it", much to the amusement of the court.

Dinny was fined two pounds with costs (*Daily News*, [Perth], 16 March 1917, p9).

Dinny treated himself to trips around the world. During his travels, he did some trap shooting in Monte Carlo and Johannesburg and performed well. There were often reports in the local newspapers as to what he was doing on his travels. At a gymnasium in Los Angeles, he was introduced to Jack Dempsey, a champion boxer. He agreed to put the gloves on for a few rounds with him. Dinny doesn't say what he did to Dempsey on this occasion!

After many years of travel and adventure, Dinny settled in Eastern Australia for a while. He returned to the Goldfields after hearing of the big nugget found in Larkinville.

In his younger days, Dinny was prominent in football, cricket, and a noted long-distance walker. He held the long walk record of sixty miles for a fifty-pound wager. This was accomplished within twenty-two hours in stages without sleep. On another occasion, he walked one-hundred miles in two and a half days from Menzies to Coolgardie on an old track. After hobbling into town at 11pm, "he had a clean-up, bought an argument and outed a fourteen stone John Hop with one of his 'bull ant biffs'" (*Sunday Times* [Perth], 1 March 1914 p1).

At sixty-three he walked a mile and a half from the Halfway to the Palace Hotel Kalgoorlie in thirteen minutes to raise money for charity. Shortly afterwards he won a half mile walk at the trotting grounds against all comers. However, his challenge to walk to Coolgardie and back (fifty miles) for a wager of twenty-five pounds was not taken up (*Kalgoorlie Miner*, 9 July 1941).

He remained in Kalgoorlie, and fortunately, he wrote the story of his life, *"Dennis O'Callaghan's Long Life and Reminiscences and adventures Throughout the World" (1941)*, which is quite an entertaining read.

Chapter Two

McCann's Duffer Rush

THE POEM BELOW WAS PUBLISHED in the *Kalgoorlie Sun* on 4 July 1895. What did McCann do to have such a poem published about him? He started a bogus 'wildcat' rush and was lucky not to be lynched.

> Hang him up as high as Haman, (i)
> Jerk him to the Devil's band;
> Let him suffer hideous tortures –
> Come, ye diggers, lend a hand.
> Let him taste the sweets of misery,
> He that brought the "mulga wire", (ii)
> Glue him well with tar and feathers,
> Cast him in a burning fire.
> Hang him up as high as Haman,
> Let it be a lesson to
> All the skulking, 'wild-cat' boomers
> Of the shiny reptile crew.

McCann's Duffer Rush

> It ain't no use argufying
> Diggers, do your duty well;
> Choke him first, then kerosene him,
> Banquet him en route for - well
> (That's a warm place.)
> String him to the nearest gum tree,
> Strike the iron while it's hot;
> Let the beggar have no mercy;
> Leave him in the sun to rot.
> Hang him up as high as Haman,
> He that sent us all astray,
> Searching round the reckless desert,
> Humping bluey all the way. iii

[You ought to feel better now after jerking that bile off your chest – Ed. M. and P.] (*Coolgardie Miner*, 4 July 1895, p3)

Infamous stories generally have many versions, and this story is no different in that regard. Some believed McCann was a notoriously lousy bushman who was prone to exaggeration when drunk. Others thought he was a liar who threatened their lives by sending them into the desert for no good reason. Whatever the truth, 'doing a McCann' became an expression in the goldfields for starting a dangerous bogus rush.

McCann was described as a big, strong Irish-Australian man born in Victoria. According to some, he was very illiterate and enjoyed a drop or two of alcohol (*Sunday Times* [Perth], 30 January 1927, p39).

Someone using the non-de plume of "Dido" published the following version of events in the *Sun* ([Kalgoorlie], 6 March 1910, p14).

McCann's Duffer Rush

In June 1895, a man called Beaglehole approached Dido in Coolgardie. He asked him if he knew of anyone who could take a whip horse to the Cardiff Castle Mine at Widgiemooltha. Dido knew of a chap camped near him called McCann who claimed to be a good bushman. He was doing nothing at the time, so he agreed to do the job. Within an hour McCann was on the road to Widgiemooltha with the horse.

McCann delivered the horse without a problem. Yet, he wasn't quite the bushman he made himself out to be as he didn't return directly to Coolgardie. He went entirely off-course and found himself near Red Hill (Kambalda), around seventy-five kilometres from Coolgardie.

At Red Hill, he found a 'shaker' and some tools in one of the gullies. He thought that someone had recently been working there. The equipment belonged to Jim Rope and his party who camped some distance away. As he could not see anyone, he had a good look around and specked a couple of pieces of alluvial. He then looked for the men and their camp. When he couldn't find them, he decided to set out for Coolgardie. He finally arrived in Coolgardie as the sun was setting - footsore and weary.

Dido was standing at the bottom of Bayley Street, near the old Freemasons when McCann arrived. McCann came up to him rather excited. Too loudly he began to tell him of the gold he had specked.

"Shut up, you old fool", Dido exclaimed. "Why, you will draw a crowd here in two ticks talking like that. There's McCallum, Smith and Chandler of the Golden Age making for us straight now."

McCann grabbed Dido's arm and said: "Let's get. I don't want any

McCann's Duffer Rush

news reporters. I am not sure of it yet."

The two men dodged the reporters. Dido decided it best to keep his eye on Mac (as he called McCann) until they both could go to the site the next day. Dido went to McCann's camp after his tea, and to his horror, McCann wasn't there. He must have gone into town. Dido searched for him until two in the morning with no luck. At 11am, he spotted him in Bayley Street 'well drunk' with a dozen or so men following him. Talking wildly, McCann emphasised to the men that he did not know the location of his find, protesting that he would let everyone know when he did.

John Marshall's book "Battling for Gold" provides another version of the events preceding the bogus rush. Marshall was secretary of the Gold Digger's Association at the time. He states that McCann was a notoriously lousy bushman with no idea of distances. He had been down south somewhere, in the direction of Lake Lefroy. On his return, he entered an unknown gully and came across extensive alluvial workings. It was raining, and the diggers were in their tents. They took him in for the night, dispensed whisky and later showed him pickle bottles filled with gold. It was an excited and alcoholic McCann that blew into Coolgardie the next night. Times were hard, and it took money to buy whiskey, but with a well-told tale of gold in pickle bottles, he was given many free drinks.

Later that day, the *Golden Age* printed a special bulletin carrying news of the find:

> We have been creditably informed that a kerosene tin filled with gold was brought into town from the new rush and everything

points to the existence of a new and extra-ordinary goldfield ... down south someway (Sun [Kalgoorlie], 8 November 1908, p11).

What happened next is detailed in the article "Over the Plates – McCann's Rush". This article repeated John Marshall's written account (*Western Mail* [Perth], 26 May 1938, p9).

The paper's special edition was quickly sold out. All over town groups of eager miners could be seen discussing the news of the sensational find of alluvial gold.

News of the find spread rapidly all over the eastern goldfields. Thousands of men poured into Coolgardie from Hannans (Kalgoorlie), White Feather (Kanowna), Black Flag, Broad Arrow, I.O.U. (Bulong), Roaring Gimlet (Goongarrie), and Menzies. Some came on foot and carried their swags, some pushed wheelbarrows, but most of them travelled in buggies, on horseback, or by camel. Parties were leaving Coolgardie at all hours of the day and night. Some were well equipped, others ill-equipped with supplies for only a few days. Some would very likely have perished through lack of water, but for some timely rain.

Chafing with delay and burning with excitement, the lack of definite information caused tempers to rise. A week of this maddening excitement passed, and there was still no real information. With many frustrated miners swarming into town, trouble was anticipated.

A crowd of angry men rushed the newspaper offices where they were given very vague answers. They got mad at the papers for publishing misleading intelligence. Yet, they did learn from them that the story of the alluvial find had originated from McCann.

As secretary of the Diggers Association, Marshall had been trying to ascertain the accuracy of the reports regarding the find. He was worried that the situation could suddenly get out of hand and people may lose their lives.

He was walking down Bayley Street when he saw a large, excited crowd farther down the street. As he drew closer, he saw that "… a number of the baser fellows, upon whom the impress of villainy, not honest labour, was stamped, were roughly using a tall man, who appeared to be much agitated and whom I learned was none other than McCann himself." He decided that it was now time to act. Raising his voice to its highest pitch, he cried out:

> Look here, boys! You know that I am John Marshall, secretary of the Western Australian Diggers' Association. Things are getting serious. Thousands of men are rolling into town. The reports published by newspapers so far appear to have no foundation in fact, and it is time something was done to end this maddening doubt and uncertainty. I am determined to take steps to locate the alleged rush and find out whether McCann's report be true or not. I shall, therefore, call a public meeting on behalf of the association this afternoon at three o'clock and the matter will then be thoroughly discussed. McCann will have to speak out and tell us what he knows when steps shall be taken to organise a party to go out with him and settle whether the find be a fraud or not. I shall take charge of McCann and see that he turns up with me to the meeting.

The crowd approved of the idea and dispersed. The local bellman was engaged to go around the town to spread the news of the forthcoming monster public meeting at Recreation Reserve.

Much to Marshall's alarm, when he woke up in the morning, McCann wasn't to be found. Fortunately for Marshall, he returned but was looking miserable. Marshall tried to ascertain from McCann what the chances were of success, but he was not pleased with McCann's response.

A large crowd of miners, storekeepers and townsfolk gathered at Recreation Reserve and at the appointed time proceedings began. A wagon was used for a rostrum. After some introductory speeches, McCann stepped up and was greeted with a storm of abuse, hisses, and derisive cheers from the immense crowd. Marshall felt sorry for the man:

> There he stood – a big, broad-shouldered, brawny man with a heavy dark moustache, compressed lips and pale cheeks. His manner was halting and undecided – he had apparently been drinking heavily and he was surrounded on all sides by angry miners, hundreds of whom believed him guilty of the greatest of all crimes, the originating of a bogus rush: and these would willingly have lent a hand to 'give a lift up' had a suitable rope and the opportunity been available.

At first, McCann was nervous and hesitant, but as he warmed to his subject, he became more confident. He denied responsibility for bringing about the rush and volunteered to lead a party to the place where he had found the gold. The crowd applauded enthusiastically. McCann spoke with such an air of candour and assurance even astute men believed he spoke the truth. At the close of the meeting, McCann was handed over to Marshall so that he would not escape.

Someone opened a subscription list, and within a short time, sufficient money was raised to equip a party to accompany McCann. Experienced bushmen; Sam Cook, Billy Kerr, Tom Connors, and Billy Brogan were chosen. They had enough supplies to last a fortnight, firearms to protect McCann with and horses were supplied by Mr Joe Matthews (*Sunday Times* [Perth], 30 Jan 1927, p.39).

The following was published in the *Coolgardie Miner* on 21 June:

THE NEW ALLUVIAL RUSH AT CARDIFF CASTLE

NEAR LAKE COWAN.

DEFINITE PARTICULARS AND ROUTE.

LEAD ONE CHAIN WIDE.

27 OZS. IN 4 DAYS WITH A SIEVE.

Mr M. McCann, an old Ballarat and Maryborough, Vic., miner, has just returned from the new alluvial field, which he prefers calling the Cardiff Castle instead of Lake Cowan, and has furnished us with the following particulars. His statement is terse and to the point, viz.:—I left here on Saturday morning last on behalf of a syndicate, to look at a reef, and arrived at the

NEW FIELD

at 7:30 on Monday morning. About forty were camped on the ground, and one man invited me to have a drink of tea. Finding I was from Coolgardie, he said I was the first from there. He then showed me about 100 pieces of shotty gold, the largest 1 oz.,17dwts., and 10dwts each, and running down to 5 and 6gms., with some fine gold. The whole was the result of four days works with a sieve. All the other men there were also doing well. The field is described as being 65 miles distant from Coolgardie and

McCann's Duffer Rush

12 miles south by east from the Norseman. The lead is over two miles from the lake and running directly towards it, where Mr McCann thinks it will widen out and become poorer in consequence. It is one chain wide, and the gold is found from the surface to a depth of 2 feet 6 inches.

THE ROUTE.

The most direct way is to proceed via Tindal's to the Sheep Bocks, thence south to Burra Burra, and thence to the Norseman, from which the new field is 12 miles distant south by east. Our informant is of opinion that there is

ROOM FOR 1,000 MEN,

and it will take from 12 months to 15 months to work out. He did not go there after the alluvial, but in connection with reefs in the locality which he had formerly been to.

***

The five men then set out on their search. Marshall had many misgivings about sending McCann to look for the alluvial find. He knew that if he were unsuccessful, the chances were ten to one that he would be shot or hanged somewhere on the road, despite the four men protecting him. This was because "there were many desperate characters who would do the job". He was weighed down with the sense of responsibility he had incurred.

When all the necessities for the trip had been loaded up on the buggies, a photograph was taken. Their departure was signalised by prolonged cheering from the crowd gathered to see them off. McCann was very confident about being able to lead the party directly to the spot where he saw some men getting good gold. They expected the trip to take at least five days as the last ten or twelve miles would be difficult for the buggy (*Coolgardie Miner*, 26 June 1895, p2).

They proceeded via Tinsdale's mine, Londonderry mine, and Horse Rock soak. They then went across the Coolgardie track to Norseman road and east to Lake Cowan. With McCann leading on foot, the party searched for two whole days. By this time the number on the trail was getting on towards a hundred men. Ugly glances were cast at McCann from time to time and suggestions of cutting off one of his ears and such like mooted. McCann's protectors had to keep a night watch to prevent something of this kind really happening.

At last McCann admitted that he could not find the spot, so the party decided to go back to Coolgardie. Cookes and Brogan took charge of McCann in the buckboard and covered him over with rugs. Billy Kerr would not take the risk of riding in the vehicle. He travelled with Connor (*Sunday Times* [Perth], 30 January 1927, p39).

Meanwhile, many alarming stories were being received about the lack of water and supplies for some of the parties in the fields. An intelligence department was organised so information could be collected from people when they returned to Coolgardie. Bulletins were posted outside of the office. The whole town was in a simmer of excitement.

At a meeting in Coolgardie on 27 June, it was decided not to send relief provisions out to the diggers in the fields. They were advised that the diggers had enough food and were only two days from town. While waiting for McCann, they were chiefly engaged in playing 'two up'. Rumours were starting that McCann had 'levanted', but these rumours were dismissed (*West Australian* [Perth], 29 June 1895, p5).

McCann's Duffer Rush

Marshall was becoming very worried about the outcome for McCann. The police rendered him every assistance. Scouts were kept night and day at the main approaches of the town to give warning of the returning party. Marshall was praying that they returned on Sunday, as the people would be soberer on that day.

Don Miller of Mullewa recalled his part of the drama in an article published in the *Western Mail's* "The Dollypot" (26 May 1938, p9).

He was carting supplies from the end of the railway line to Coolgardie for Jack Murray, a store-keeper. On reaching Coolgardie, Bill Weston approached him and asked him to take a party of prospectors out. Jack Murray also asked him to take goods out for a store he intended to establish at the new rush, which he agreed to do. His team was the first to return, as they got word that McCann's alleged find could not be located. He was then approached to go back with provisions for a relief team, but word arrived they were on their way back. He claims they were quite desperate and if the crowd had got McCann "he could have said a long farewell".

McCann's return journey was halted near Widgiemooltha by a rope stretched across the track. An angry mob of between four-hundred and five-hundred men surrounded them. They threatened retribution to McCann for having led them on a fruitless search. Somebody noticed a movement under the rugs in the buggy, where poor McCann was blubbering like a child. The crowd demanded that he should be handed to them for treatment.

The situation was tense, violence could erupt at any moment. The party had sworn that they would protect McCann and were determined to do so. Billy Kerr stood up in the sulky and made a speech, telling the maddened crowd to refrain from violence. Half a dozen of the cooler-headed men who knew the party managed to calm down the group. Fortunately, the party was able to proceed back to Coolgardie (*Sunday Times* [Perth], 30 January 1927, p39).

Someone on the party with McCann later told Marshall that he repeatedly requested a revolver to commit suicide. They were determined to prevent him from doing so, as well as to shield him from the vengeance of others.

Marshall's prayers were answered, as the party arrived at six o'clock on Sunday night. His protectors managed to save him and were very relieved when they finally came back to Coolgardie. Every available police officer was sent to protect McCann.

News of the party's return spread through the town and in a short time Bayley Street was crowded. McCann wanted to address the crowd, but fortunately, he was prevented from doing so for his own protection.

It was agreed that a report should be drawn up showing the route travelled and the results obtained. Marshall was concerned that he may become a martyr during the hour it took to complete the report. When it was finished, it was read out to the expectant crowd. Marshall advised the report found that:

> ... the alleged great gold discovery was a cruel hoax – that not an ounce of gold had actually been discovered: that thousands of pounds spent, and the lives of hundreds of men were endangered by the babblings of a drunken man, to whom credence had been given and authority lent by journalists who ought to have known better.

McCann's Duffer Rush

Marshall continued:

> Then occurred a scene which positively baffles description. The excitement which had been pent up for weeks burst forth in a torrent of mingled howls of wrath, execration and vengeance. Cries of 'Bring McCann out!', 'String him up!', 'Pull his liver out', 'tear him from limb to limb!', came from men in the crowd.

A man accused Marshall of hiding McCann, and the crowd then threatened to pull his house down. Marshall knew he had to calm the largest crowd he had ever seen on the goldfields. The fury of the mob was rising to madness. He stepped up onto the crate with a feeling he was on trial for his life. He narrated the steps he had taken to serve the public interest and appealed to the diggers "not to be stirred up to deeds of violence by the pimps, parasites and spielers who were in the crowd". He blamed the newspapers for publishing sensational reports without first checking their accuracy. He urged the crowd not to create a disturbance, reminding them that the police were protecting McCann. He begged them not to take vengeance on a poor, drunken man.

The crowd seemed to accept Marshall's pleas somewhat grudgingly until another man got up and incited them against the offending newspapers. They decided to vent their feelings on one of the newspaper offices nearby.

Some police and law-abiding citizens formed a cordon around the building to prevent them from entering. The angry mob broke some windows and damaged a part of the outside building, but nothing more serious occurred.

According to a witness named John Micklejohn, a few policemen on the spot did their utmost to restrain them, but they were overwhelmed by force of numbers. Meiklejohn wrote:

> Then the commanding figure of Warden Finnerty appeared, and all eyes were on him. He was hatless, and his brown eyes flashed indignation as he ordered the mob to disperse, threatening them with the utmost rigour of the law if they disobeyed. He said "I represent the Government and I will not permit any person to take the law into his own hands". Not a man opposed him. The delinquents immediately realised the Warden's magnetic influence, and, like naughty children, they peaceably melted away. It was a splendid example of the Warden's personality – a victory of one fearless man against an unruly mob (*Western Mail* [Perth], 1937).

McCann's Duffer Rush

The next day McCann thanked Marshall for saving his life, and the police escorted McCann out of town.

A few days after McCann left town, many men with their slow-moving horse and camel teams returned to Coolgardie from Widgiemooltha. The cavalcade entered town preceded by a camel bearing gallows with a life-sized effigy of McCann. When bystanders saw the hated figure swinging from side to side, they joined the procession into town.

The crowd stopped in front of the post office and the windowless newspaper office across the road. A few of the men then lit a bonfire in the street. As the fire blazed high amid cheers and shouts from the onlookers, McCann's effigy was saturated with oil and thrown into the centre. When the dummy had almost burnt out, it was dragged from the fire. Police managed to overcome attempts to hurl the effigy into the newspaper office. As the bonfire died down, the crowd gradually dispersed, and the curtain fell on the last act of the McCann drama.

A man who travelled with McCann on his journey to Coolgardie in 1893 on the 'sluggish and unsafe' steamship *Nemesis*, wrote his impression of McCann:

> McCann was quite the loudest and most prominent circumstance on board. If there were any loud, aggressive noises to be made, McCann made them. If there was any person claiming a right to argue as to the boss-ship of the crazy old scow, McCann was the one and only. When the tucker was dealt out in buckets and tubs at the ill-manned gallery, it was McCann who directed as to who should be served first or last. But it was mere good-natured bluff and noise-joke, McCann being as soft-hearted and susceptible as

an average woman. Big and burly of physique, and possessing an enormous voice, Mac would strike the crowd dumb with a threatening roar and the next minute would lumber away with some fruit ullaged from the cargo for some poor sick devil who couldn't fight for food.

Down at Colreavy's dam at Fly Flat on the Sunday of arrival writer saw and heard McCann order a score of swampers to stand back until called upon to get their water in turn. And half-way back to his own camp (a mile and a half) he stopped and poured every drop from his own bag into that of an old greybeard who was late in getting towards the gabbie. Regarding sending men to a duffer rush, McCann wouldn't do it intentionally and was probably worked into it (The Sun [Kalgoorlie], 3 April 1910, p15).

I believe it fitting to end this story with an article published in the *Sunday Times*:

McCANN'S RUSH

McCann, of the famous "McCann's, Rush", the story of which has been printed and reprinted so often and so voluminously, is now a permanent resident of Darwin. It is a long time since Mac was the centre of the famous disturbance in Bayley-street Coolgardie when a newspaper office was threatened with demolition and an editor with annihilation. It was 1895, but ever since the story is raked up in varied forms. One phase of the historic rumpus is neglected by most of the historians, and that is that the genuine old battlers, the men who chased the weight in '92, '93 '94 and '95, are now firmly convinced that McCann really did see some rich specimens and alluvial slugs down in the country which he tried, vainly to relocate under escort. There seems to be not the slightest doubt that it was either at the present Larkinville or near it that Mac was shown something on which he built his story, for there is no doubt good gold did come from that part in the early days, two men actually coming in a few weeks later from there, probably thinking they had exhausted the whole of the ground and going East with a considerable amount of the precious metal. In those days there was no need to declare the quantity of gold, and as dealers existed all over the place and the Mints asked no questions except, merely official ones, gold could be bought and sold almost anywhere. There are now two McCann's, one at Larkinville and another up in the wheat lands near Burracoppin who being old Coolgardie men, have often been accused of being the original "McCann of the Rush". The real Mac, now of Darwin, has now practically been proved right in his statement of 35 years ago ("Peeps at People" *Sunday Times* [Perth],19 July 1931, p7).

[ii] From the book of Esther. Haman wanted to hang Esther's uncle Mordicai to make a spectacle of him, so he built a very large, high gallows. He got caught framing Mordicai so King Ahasuerus had him hanged on his own gallows.

[iiii] Mulga Wire is the gossip network in the outback

[iii] Carrying one's bundle; tramp

Chapter Three

When Kanowna was Young

KANOWNA IS GHOST-TOWN nineteen kilometres east of Kalgoorlie. In its early years, the town was known as White Feather. Jerry McAuliffe said this name came about after a fight in the first rush between two prospectors, Ahern and Saunders. They decided whoever won the fight also won ownership of the claim they were disputing (*Western Mail* [Perth], 16 December 1898, p123). Saunders did not know that Aherns was a 'top notcher' of the game, so he soon 'had Saunders to the mother earth'. Thinking it was a fluke, Saunders stood up and was quickly floored again. He then ran off leaving Ahern in possession of the claim. A witness named Monaghan retold the story of the fight from camp to camp, and he always ended the story saying that Saunders had 'shown the white feather'. The next day everyone called the place the White Feather (*Kalgoorlie Miner*, 12 October 1897, p2).

Another slightly different version is:

The fighters were not evenly matched; one was a big man and the other quite small. However, after the fight had been in progress for some time, the big man admitted defeat and told his small opponent to keep the claim as it was not worth fighting for! Meanwhile, the other diggers had gathered around to watch the fight, and one of them, an Irish man named Monaghan called out as the scrap ended. "The big fellow has shown the white feather, we'll call this place The White Feather", and for some time afterwards Monaghan made it his business to advise newcomers that the name of the field was 'The White Feather' (Compton 15).

There are a few different versions of when, who and how the first gold discovery was made at Kanowna. The dates of the gold find also vary. Even McAuliffe gives slightly different versions. In December 1896, in the *Western Argus* of 17 December, he implies he was prospecting on his own when he first found gold. There is no mention of others in his party finding gold. His later interview printed in the *Kalgoorlie Miner* on 19 October 1897, provides more detail. The latter version is like other people's recollection of events. Their combined accounts are detailed below.

Jerry McAuliffe, Mick Breen, R Gwynne, and W Bowler found the first gold near Kanowna on 8 August 1893 (McAuliffe said this occurred at the beginning of September). These prospectors had experience from Queensland, New Guinea, and Western Australia. They left the area on their Brumbies when they heard rumours of a gold discovery by the Moher brothers at I.O.U (Bulong).

McAuliffe had a reputation as being worth chasing, so two men, Finn and Prendergras, followed his tracks. The two parties were not on friendly terms, one was angry and annoyed, the other watchful and alert.

One day both parties boiled their midday billies on the flats. After dinner, Breen picked up a good piece of gold (6dwt) when bringing in the horses. He was only a few yards away from the camp of the followers, but he managed to keep this find a secret from them. As they found little and were determined to shake off the spies, they decided to leave. They went to I.O.U but didn't have success there. They then went to Victoria Springs which is two-hundred miles due eastward from Kanowna. Victoria Springs was one of explorer Giles' watering places. They finally got gold near Peaks Find. Here the party disbanded, but McAuliffe and Breen returned to Kanowna to search the area again.

Meanwhile, two other prospectors, Tom (Tassy) O'Connor and Jim Hilder, had worked out their claims in Broad Arrow, so they left with the intention of prospecting the Mt. Yule country. The first night out they camped at a claypan about ten miles north of Kalgoorlie where they met Percy Larkins, his small Aboriginal boy named Monkey, McAuliffe and several others.

As O'Connor didn't have a mate, he went with Monkey out to the east to prospect. Monkey discovered a rich reef later known as McAuliffe's Reward and Tassy found gold-bearing leaders on what was afterwards known as Red Hill. When Tassy returned to camp, it was agreed that he, Jim Hilder, Percy Larkin, Dave Heppingstone, Jerry McAuliffe, and Mick Breen should go mates. Unfortunately, poor Monkey wasn't included in this arrangement and is rarely mentioned (*Western Mail* [Perth], 16 December 1898).

McAuliffe said they found 'splendid gold'. They paid one-pound per acre for the lease and called it Day Dawn.

There is an account in 'The Dollypot" from J.E.T of Nedlands (*Western Mail* [Perth], 27 November 1941, p43). In it, he states that Percy Larkins rode throughout the night to J.E.T.'s camp in Broad Arrow to advise him of his party's find a few days prior. J.E.T arrived in Kanowna with Ted McGrath and Jack Samuels the next day, and they camped at Tassy's camp.

Samuels was packing water from a claypan to the west and Monkey was packing water from one about ten miles south. The water was filthy, and when cleaned with kopi it yielded about half water and half sediment. J.E.T says the two things he remembers most about Kanowna was the bad water and Monkey. He said the following about Monkey:

> He was about ten years of age, and very small so that when he was hunched up on a horse with a man's coat wrapped around him, and his feet tucked in the stirrup leathers, he looked very much like his namesake. All the same, he was a game little kid and generally led three horses loaded with water (Western Mail [Perth], 27 November 1941).

I have tried to find more information about Monkey, but all I could ascertain is that he came from the North-West of the State. There was a sensational murder trial in 1905 at Marble Bar where two Aboriginal men, Monkey and Toby, were eventually acquitted of their charges. They were accused of spearing, murdering and dismembering a prospector, but the bones the Aboriginals led the police to were Aboriginal. No doubt the police interrogation methods resulted in a false confession and false statements from their friends. Unfortunately, the two acquitted were not heard of again. No investigation to locate them occurred, so we will never know if they just left the area or were murdered themselves because of the trial and acquittal. The reporting of the murders was very sensational, they even reported cannibalism occurred. I cannot confirm that the boy and man known as Monkey are the same, but the ages fit, and both spoke good English, so it is possible.

J.E.T also advised that Tassy went to a rush in British Guiana, via Rome, Paris and London and that all he got there was a good dose of malaria. He arrived back in the West in time to get a good claim in the Kanowna Deep Lead.

Water had to be fetched from Broad Arrow, over twenty-five miles from the camp and supplies soon became unavailable. Supplies were even scarce in Coolgardie due to the increased population. According to J.E.T., Magpies and Crows were on the menu on at least one occasion.

By July 1894, McAuliffe sold the claim for £6,500 to Lord Percy Douglas, for floatation in London (*South Australian Register*, 25 July 1894, p6). They called it McAuliffe's Reward, even though a Government reward was not given to McAullife. The mine was also known as the White Feather Reward Mine.

An immense amount of surface gold was taken until June 1894. At the end of 1893, the real rush began when two brothers found the Chignly auriferous body of conglomerate, known locally as cement.

A rush of over two-hundred men then took place. Several leases were pegged following the first rush. These were mostly on a long line later known as the Main Reefs Line. Between the northern and southern sections were two areas where gold was found at a shallow depth, most of it embedded in the cement-like substance.

Micklejohn and Cottingham took up the Golden Crown leases, which carried a reef with a rich outcrop. In 1894, this was pegged out for an Adelaide syndicate for £11,000 cash (*South Australian Register*, 9 Nov 1894). Bissenberger took out the Main Reef leases which he sold to a Perth Company. Backed by a small syndicate from Adelaide, in November 1893, Otto Shriven pegged out Nemesis. He worked it and proved it contained three distinct reefs. It was the wealthiest mine at that time.

It was estimated that over £80,000 worth of gold was taken out before the end of the year. Maori Bill and his mate took £10,000 from their claims.

The first condenser in the district was erected by 'German Charlie'. It was located on the borders of the nearest 'lake' on Kurnalpi road. (Afterwards, this was the scene of the sacred nugget rush caused by Father Long.) Mrs German Charlie was the first white woman in the district.

Even in these early days, the alluvial question (though not under that name), was harassing the owners of reefing properties. A vast amount of trouble and bad blood was caused by the encroachment of the diggers on the man reef line of leases. Finally, owing to a mistake of the manager of the Golden Eagle, this property was left jumpable, and on behalf of a Perth syndicate, Mr F. J. McManus promptly availed himself of the opportunity.

This ground was finally floated as the Golden Cement Company. However, the original diggers had left very few pickings within the pegs, and the company got little return. The property was finally let to tributers, Murray, Cray, and party, who completed a crushing of 500 tons at the Shamrock Co.'s Griffin mills.

In the Red Hill area to the north of the town where the alluvial workings were, hundreds of men screened the surface dirt looking for nuggets. They had to make their own fun, and a reporter called Job Trotter describes a Saturday night's entertainment in December 1894:

> The attraction of the night was the open-air concert. Facing the light of a store were about 130 of the residents, chiefly miners of the district, some seated on boxes, cases or anything available, others squatting in the dust and others standing.
>
> The M.C. introduced the first item, a song, then a recitation, then more songs, more recitations, stump speeches, step dances – the stage being a fruit case which answered very well. Occasionally the entertainment was varied by about between friends with the gloves ...
>
> At halftime, a collection was taken up to help a man with his son's funeral expenses, and four pounds was raised.
>
> The entertainment continued up till nearly midnight when the evening's amusement was concluded by a buck set of quadrilles. Strict instructions were issued to the gentlemen to swing their partners thoroughly (no heel taps) but not immodestly.
>
> The dance raged fast and furious; now you saw the dancers, now you didn't, but the culminating point was the sixth figure. Partners were lost, stolen or strayed: I am told some have not been found

yet whilst others are still turning up.

In the quarter of a century, I have spent on various goldfields of different colonies, I have never met an assemblage of men enjoying themselves more thoroughly, respectfully and innocently.

Another account of early Kanowna is in a letter published in the *Queenslander* on 17 March 1894:

Dear —, —Got in from the Feather on Tuesday morning last, fearfully tired, having made one stretch of the whole distance (forty-eight miles). I left on Monday at noon and arrived on Tuesday morning at about 9 - not bad walking. Of course, I had only my blankets, water, and tucker bags for impedimenta. As soon as I arrived, I inquired for the post and was astonished to receive three letters from you amongst others. The mystery was quickly solved when I saw one was opened and bearing innumerable postmarks of such a recent date as Ist October. 'Tis a wonderful country, whose coat of arms should be a sleepy lizard in repose, while the motto should be - unquam dormio, or ne varietur, or, best of all, 'we are content'. The Western Australia postal arrangements are of the go-as-you-please-dot-and-carry-one style. While on the postal grievance, I must tell you what a Government official here told me concerning his experience therewith. His wife was in Perth, and on his arrival at the Cross he wrote to her and posted it just before leaving. A week after his arrival in Coolgardie he inquired for his letters and got his own handed out to him. What do you think of that, now? Well, I suppose you want an account of what has taken place up to date since my last to you. There is nothing very startling to narrate; some of the incidents have caused as many a smile after a happy issue therefrom, although, at the time the prospect looked serious enough.

Well, on the day after writing you last, Mr Barney (the dog), and I set out for the Feather, humping our drums, of course. The 'White Feather' (why so-called I could never ascertain) is about eighteen miles north-east from Hannan's, and some good patches had been found there, as well as some fine reefs, and that is why we started out for it. We got to Hannan's and had to wait a couple of days to find the storekeeper, with whom we had left our flour when we had to retreat on account of the water giving out. We found that there were very few stores indeed in the camp, and only about 100 men, all told, on the field - reefers, businessmen, and alluvial diggers. There are two hotels going up in this place, and a trooper is also quartered here. We found the storeman had sold our flour as the mice were so bad. So, after getting the equivalent, we set out on Thursday morning, and after travelling through flat, uninteresting country, though of a much better description than any we had seen since leaving Northam, and, passing skeletons of camels and horses, and a broken-down waggon, reached our destination that same evening. It took us all the next day to get our tent fixed, and shade built over it, and make a canvas water tank to hold about 70 gallons of water - this was to store water in so as to be prepared for any emergency. We had been informed by the usual liar than any other liar was a liar who denied that there were plenty of stores at the Feather and that there was 'whips of stuff' in the provision line, and water only 3d per gallon and any amount of it. We found there was a very little flour, tea, sugar, preserved potatoes, and some tinned herrings - oh, and some jam; and water 9d., and only 800 at that for about 100 men. On Sunday the potatoes were all done, and we had to live on black-bream bait - dough and herring for a couple of days, when we changed our diet to herrings straight on account of the flour being done.

Paisleys team came in just as the fish were all done and a famine setting in and brought out some fish, floor, some scraps of bacon and some mutton hams of a more or less doubtful aroma, and we had a 'blow out' I can assure you. It is amazing to see the way the 'shopping' is done here. The shop is the cleanest spot the teamster can find handy; the goods are tipped on to this, and the men crush in, take what they can get in the scramble, and then wait their turn to pay the teamster. I never yet heard of any complaint about things being taken and not paid for. The teamster would be busily engaged in weighing the gold, referring to his ready reckoner, while the diggers were scrambling and helping themselves to his goods. We secured 60 gallons of water and stored it. On the 14th all the water in the tanks was done, and the carter had to go into Hannan's for some while his condenser was being fixed. (By, tanks I always refer to galvanised iron ones, of a holding capacity for about 600 gallons. Coolgardie is the only place with dams, except of course along the track from there to the Cross. One of the Coolgardie dams, the police dam, is on top of a hill for some reason or other; it would make a good barracks or fortress, being exceptionally dry). Well, let me see - I was telling you about the water at the Feather. The day the carter was away the men had to go without till he turned up at night with 200 gallons; price 2s per gallon! On the 15th there was nothing in the camp save jam and rice, and on that, all hands had to makeshift till the team came in on the evening of the 20th. A wholesome dietary scale with a vengeance and would no doubt suit dyspeptic. The 21st was Sunday and ended a week of semi-starvation, terrible heat, cloudless, unpitying blue sky - not a breath of wind any part of it. I never in my life before experienced anything like it for flies, and the mice were an awful nuisance at night. On Friday and Saturday, not a man was at work on account of the heat and, I suppose, weakness. Somebody 'took us down' for all but a gallon or so of our water; the diggers were in a great state about it, and if the culprit could be found matters would be lively for him. By the team that came in on the 20th was a note from B--, telling me to come in straight away, so after feeding all day Sunday on tinned meat and preserved potatoes, I set out on Monday afternoon for Coolgardie, which I reached on Tuesday morning, as I informed you above. The water at the Feather before the condenser was brought in (only 200 gallons every other day) was grand; it was 'soak' water, and full of animalcules, which as soon as they had laid their eggs were no further interested in subsequent proceedings, so floated on their watery bier, as Milton puts it, thereby causing the said watery bier to distil an aroma of a most disagreeable nature, and the flavour was in keeping with it. This would last about eight or ten days, when the heirs, executors, or assigns of the deceased would emerge from their incubator and dutifully 'scoff' the remains of their relatives, and the watery bier would become wholesome and sweet-smelling again, until the time came for the new lot to become entailed or entrailled estate, and the performance would take place over again, to cholera or hydatid music.

Just before we got to the Feather, the blacks raided the camp while the men were away at work. The diggers - mostly overlanders from Queensland and one or two Africanders, but all real hard cases and real grit - will make them sit up if they sight them again. After the performance a couple did come back, and a long thin Africander and overlander, called Long Charlie, coaxed one of them up and then went to split him down with his prospecting dish, but the nigger ducked, and Charlie slung his foot at him with much effect, and then fired his dish after him, nearly scalping him. The men roar again when they tell about it and describe the celerity with which that nigger became endowed with Charlie pursuing him.

There are some grand reefs at the Feather, but nearly all the country has been taken up in selections by representatives of English syndicates. One reef above the main works, just before we left, was yielding 1lb. of metal between two for the dollying. Whoever runs these fields down is an ass. Bayley's is the deepest down on the field, and at 120ft. is as good as on top. There are not so very many reefs here that do not show gold on the surface, and all the prospecting these reefs get about here is with the butt of the pick. I am talking of reefs that show above the surface, for the idea of digging and prospecting for a reef, unless, of course, good alluvial was found close by, would be scouted, so that all the trial the reef gets is by having a couple of pieces knapped off it and examined to see if it shows 'gold' or only colours; if 'gold', it is taken up; if only 'colours', it is prospected a bit to see if there is 'gold' in it, and if after a few days 'gold' is not got it is thrown up. Should the reef not be obliging enough to show even 'colours', the prospector, like the gentleman -mentioned in the Scriptures (I forget his name), passes by and says it is not worth wasting time over. There are hundreds of miles of hundreds of lines of reef here, nearly all of which are highly gold-bearing, as far as present developments can testify to. But some people, after seeing Bayley's, would decry even a 20oz reef 20ft or even 200ft in width. Every day we hear of new developments, and the only comment is – 'Well, I'm blowed! Didn't think that show much account anyway, what does she dolly?'; 'Oh! Only battery stone', & etc.

The first businesses were built near the cement area. The following is an account of setting up the first bank in Kanowna by a bank clerk named Thomas Harkness. He came to Kanowna from Perth under instructions from his employer. Upon arrival, he sought out the storekeeper who was looking after his safe and stationary that the bank had sent.

> I found this storekeeper had very neatly stowed my safe in the front part of his 14x12 foot tent and he suggested I should use

about three-foot square of his box made counter for my bank business, while he sold tinned oysters, tobacco, tin dishes and so on, over the balance.

In the politest language I told him he was mad, and with the help of willing hands soon had the safe outside. No township had yet been surveyed, so one bit of ground was as good as another, and as the storekeeper was close to the wonderful cement lead producing the gold, that seemed the place for me.

Harkness sought the aid of a man with an axe who cut eight poles from the scrub close by. They then stuck these into the ground around the safe. Harkness purchased some hessian from the storekeeper, and he and the clerk wrapped it around the poles and covered in the top. They then made a counter from wooden boxes and covered it with oilcloth.

The final touch was the door:

How proud was I of the door? You can understand the dignified appearance with a big chain through a hole and round one of the poles, fastened with a big padlock.

You cannot very well have a bank without a door to open at 10am and close at 3pm, even if you could lift up the side of the mansion and walk in that way ... (King)

Late in 1895, the businesses were moved to a newly surveyed townsite about one kilometre away. It was done by Surveyor Hamilton. The bank mentioned above was replaced with a more substantial building of wood and iron. Mr John De Baun built the first hotel of which Mr J. Johnston was the manager. Mr W. Bathe opened the first store, and he became Mayor in 1897 (*Western Mail* [Perth], 16 Dec 1898). By 1896 there were 230 houses, a population of 1,250 and a good sanitary system of thirty latrines up on the lead.

Early in November 1896, George Simm, Arthur Greeson, and Harry Watt began prospecting the area west of the Fitzroy Goldmining Companies lease. It had previously been worked over by dryblowers. They extracted 'fair gold' from their shallow workings. Their workings developed into a trench that went through the bedrock. Under the bedrock, they discovered another alluvial layer that was rich in gold. The first dish they washed off contained 540 grams of gold (*Western Mail* [Perth], 16 December 1898, p123).

For the first few weeks, they were content with dollying the cement and putting it through the shaker. In eight weeks they produced about one-hundred ounces of gold. They then decided to send a trial crushing to the Leviathon Battery in Kalgoorlie. This was because they were losing fine gold and they could not crush the gold in the hard iron-stone. The Leviathon Battery was the only public crusher near Kanowna at the time.

The results of forty-two ounces far exceeded their expectations, especially because they had picked a large quantity of gold out of the cement while it was being bagged. They sent their second crushing to the White Feather Reward which had recently opened to the public. The results were disappointing, only forty ounces for the thirty ton of cement. For the third crushing, they sent forty-four tons to the Nemesis battery and received eighty-two ounces. This was on top of the one-hundred ounces they had already picked out during bagging. The next fourteen-ton parcel returned ninety-eight ounces, not including the two-hundred ounces that were picked out during bagging. In September and the daily average increased to over ten ounces via dollying (*Coolgardie Miner,* 15 April 1898 p6).

Nearby claim holders also found they were on the same lead which ran in a westerly direction. By June 1897, the rich finds became public. Unpegged ground in this area was quickly pegged. Other leads were soon found, the richest of them being the Moonlight, Q.E.D., Wilson's Gully and the North Lead, which is described in an old geological report:

> The North Lead lies in an old watercourse carved out of the older rocks and has been proved not merely a simple isolated run of auriferous gravel, but part of a series of old stream deposits ... the deposits filing the old watercourse naturally vary somewhat in different portions. They consist first of a variable thickness of surface loam etc., succeeded by ironstone gravels partly cemented in places by kaolin and oxide or iron into solid rock. Beneath this lies a bed, or beds or particularly pure kaolin, 'pug', and varying thickness of pebbly quartz wash. The ultimate derivation of gold in the North Lead is from the quartz veins and lodes.

If a man pegged his claim above one of these deep leads, or old streams, he usually found good gold. Those who were offline got little or nothing at all. The gold-bearing clay became known as the Kanowna Pug. Because of the extremely sticky nature of the pug, it was hard to extract the gold from it. Many methods were used, but none proved successful (Compton 15).

In 1912, two brothers claimed they had found a method with to extract the gold from the pug. They did a demonstration of the extraction method with their specially erected treatment plant. The treatment plant was an iron tank. They put pug from the lead into it with a mix of secret chemicals. Water from the shaft was added, and the whole lot was stirred vigorously. More water and chemicals were added, and when the washing-off process was finished, the brothers collected the residue at the bottom of the tank. They panned it off in front of the interested crowd. The amount of gold they recovered from the small amount of pug astounded the spectators.

The brothers advised the eager crowd that they intended to form a Company to construct a plant that would extract the gold on a big scale. They quickly collected money from the future shareholders, and after packing twenty tonnes of pug, they left for Melbourne. Unfortunately for the new shareholders, they were never seen again (Compton 16) (*Daily News* [Perth] 13 February 1912, p1).

During the rush of October 1897, a reporter paid his five-shilling fare to travel from Kalgoorlie to Kanowna on a crowded Cobb & Co coach. As he jolted over the bumps on his dusty 2 ½ hour journey, he saw carts and wagons carrying various goods. There were also many men on foot carrying their swags. One coffee-stall proprietor had loaded his kiosk, four passengers and their luggage onto a trolley and was carting it out to Kanowna.

On his arrival, the journalist had lunch at Tom Doyle's Kanowna Hotel. He commented that the place was quite civilised, with ice and fresh vegetables delivered there daily. Tassy O'Connor guided him to the site of the rush, about one kilometre away. The journalist wrote:

> Just past the cemetery (the old one), we saw windlasses here, there, and everywhere. Here was a man panning off the wash while their men worked with puddling machines.
>
> Then the cry of 'Fish Ho' was heard and the trader was finding his way in and out of the various camps. Fresh eggs and butter were also sold in the same manner.

The reporter considered that there was a great deal of gold being taken from the leads. It was difficult to arrive at the exact amount taken as many of the diggers were leaving with their gold or cashing it in at stores or hotels.

Another Eastern State's journalist, May Vivienne, visited the town in November 1897. She was gathering material for her book *"Travels in Western Australia"*. However, that was not all she gathered, as everywhere she went she was presented with a 'nice little nugget' from mine managers and diggers. Of Kanowna she later wrote:

> I saw with my own eyes the enormous richness of the field and if I never saw another alluvial rush, I shall consider I was in luck when I saw Kanowna.

> I was amazed, not only by the number of tents and 'bough houses', the thousands of windlasses at work, the thousands of men with tin dishes washing the ore for gold, the thousands of cradles being rocked for the same purpose but at the thousands of men rushing in all directions in a state of wild excitement.

May reported that Simms and Gresson had taken out £10,000 worth of gold from their claim and their neighbours, Morris, Long and party had extracted 15,550 grams of gold from sixty tonnes of cement. They also obtained 6,220 grams by panning. Tassy O'Connor, Tom Doyle and party made a fortune from their claim, the Arctic Circle. She witnessed three buckets containing 9,330 grams of gold hauled to the surface. "There was great excitement of the lead that day" she wrote.

Towards the end of 1897, Diggers soon realised that one of the rich, deep leads was dipping down towards the four-hectare cemetery reserve. They sought permission to mine within its boundaries. After much deliberation, a few graves were fenced off, and the cemetery became available for pegging. Pegging was to begin at 2.30pm on a Friday. That day the crowd around the cemetery fence grew to roughly 3,000. One-third of them were intent on pegging claims, which was approximately fifty men per available claim. Armed with pegs and a pick or shovel, they jostled for a good position and waited.

Sergeant Smith rode to the centre of the cemetery with a white handkerchief in one hand and a watch in the other. All eyes were focused on him as the last few minutes, then seconds ticked away. He raised his handkerchief and as soon as he quickly lowered it, the crowd let out a roar and scrambled over the fence into the cemetery. Afterwards, the warden had quite a task sorting out the claims and the disputes that arose from over-pegging.

On the 21 October 1897, the *Kalgoorlie Western Argus* reported:

> Cobb & Co sent three coaches out today with 53 passengers, besides which numbers of men are constantly arriving here, attracted by the rich alluvial cement deposits on the Fitzroy level. Two hundred men must have arrived here during the day, and some 800 men must now be located on the cement lead. I strongly advise others to await developments and until the lead is traced beyond Gardiner's. This level in some parts is pegged 10 men's claims in width. Business is likely to be overdone.
>
> The council are taking every measure in following out the suggestions thrown out by your correspondent in looking after the sanitary condition of the new cement rush. The sudden rush of people means that extra and scattered accommodation, and at once, otherwise, the consequence will be most serious. The Government should step in and assist the council with a grant to

cope with the threatened serious outlook of things.

It is reported that another rich deposit has been made in the main shaft of the White Feather Main Reef whilst stoping back from the 1000ft level. A rich chute was met with a candle box of rich specimens, carrying about 100oz of gold, was taken out and alleged to be dispatched to Kalgoorlie. This mine is now running 20 head of stamps.

By 1897 Kanowna was an average sized mining town. Four hotels and several sly-grog shops catered for the men's thirsts. The first of two breweries had already been built. When a hotel was advertised for sale in 1898, they claimed it earned five-hundred pounds per week. The journalist remarked that "no doubt such business is better than a good claim" (*The Goldfields Mining Chronicle*, 14 April 1898, p2).

In May of 1897, the town was lit by electricity. The lights were powered by 'an erratic oil engine', and they flickered at the termination of the four main streets. In September, contractors Smith & Timms began constructing the railway line between Kalgoorlie and Kanowna. By June 1898 it was completed at the cost of £42,000. By December that year, it was the most profitable portion of the railway system in the Colony (*Western Mail*, [Perth],16 Dec 1898).

Several of the buildings, notably Mr Wilson Dunn's and Mr Host Cutbush hotels, was built of white stone from a local quarry. This rock was in high demand in Kalgoorlie, where much of it was sent (*Western Mail*, [Perth],16 Dec 1898).

In November 1897, Mr H Jerger reported on the deep leads works:

> Upwards of 3000 men are working along the line for a mile and a half getting gold. Of course, the majority of men have met with

disappointment through having sunk away from the wash" (*Coolgardie Miner,* 16 November 1897, p7).

The town clerk in 1898, Mr A. L. Tait was also secretary for the local Race Club. Kanowna was renowned for owning one of the best racecourses in the colony. £350 was spent on it during 1898 and 1899.

In 1898 there were two hospitals. Dr G. Havard Brown was the resident medical officer of the Government hospital. He married Miss May McCleod, who was the first matron. The second hospital stood close by and was operated by the Miners Sick and Accident Fund Committee until it was taken over as a private hospital by Dr Ewing (*Western Mail,* [Perth], 16 Dec 1898). During November 1901, there were seven births, one marriage and five deaths (*Kalgoorlie Western Argus,* 10 Dec 1901, p10).

In 1901 there was a limited number of condensers in the district for water. As such, the government dam was the primary water source for the residents. There was only one small pump connected with the dam, and the process of filling the tanks of the numerous carters was a prolonged one (*Kalgoorlie Western Argus,* 10 Dec 1901, p10).

Evening lectures were popular entertainment for the residents. The library was used for this purpose. On the 28th December 1909, an address was given by Reverend Wyrill on "Evolution and Life." It was reported that:

> The speaker said that the intellectual temper of the age was scientific and gave as the essential qualities of a scientific mind the faculties of perception, imagination and humility. Having defined the relation between knowledge, science and philosophy, the speaker sketched the history and meaning of the theory of

evolution and concluded by pointing out that the intellectual and social provinces of life were under the domain of evolutionary law.

The next lecture was on Tuberculosis by Dr Holland, so the lectures obviously covered a wide range of topics (*Kalgoorlie Western Argus*, 28 December 1909, p19).

Fairs were also held. This humorous account of the Anglican Fair of 1902 was provided by "The Pelican" in the *Sun* (4 May 1902, p4):

> ... was productive of at least one thrilling incident, which is still being discussed throughout Pugtown. Never since the time of Father Long's mysterious nugget has public excitement been so keen, and the episode to be related easily ranks next in importance to that momentous epoch in Kanowna history. Few reasonable people would imagine that the comparative merits of two cats would set staid, sober-minded, religious people quarrelling and hurling fierce defiances at each other, would, in fact, cause a parson and a bank official to spar around one another with blood-thirsty motives. Such is the harrowing circumstance I have to narrate. It appears that in the parson's household there exists a wondrous feline which bears the title of 'Golden Hair', while a local Hebe is the proud possessor of another cat which has been dubbed 'De Wet', the owner being a pro-Boer. Though there were several other tabbies engaged in the cat competition run at the fair, the attention of the public became centred on the two felines mentioned. The most Perfect Cat was indicated by popular vote, and as the time approached for the closing of the poll crowds of diorite-breakers from the Main Reef, led by Long Tom, began to plank their money on 'De Wet'. The admirers of the parson's cat responded with equal gameness, and public feeling ran high. Things were going pretty smoothly until the bank official aforesaid made some slighting remarks about 'Golden Hair',

which caused the reverend gentleman to utter the word 'ass' in a loud, decisive tone. "Do you call me an ass?" demanded the banker, nearly exploding with rage. "Yes," replied the parson, with a fierce gleam in his eye, "and a double distilled fool as well, so take that". They then began to peel off with great determination, but Long Tom rushed in wildly excited, and in a masterly manner prevented a conflict. Some people are talking of presenting him with a testimonial for his rare presence of mind. The fierce animosity occasioned by the De Wet-Golden Hair incident is likely to burst into flame at any moment, so the police are up to their eyes in business watching the parson and his ferocious opponent.

From the various reports it is difficult to arrive at an accurate figure of the population of Kanowna, but at its height in 1898, it is estimated that between 12,000 to 15,000 lived in and around the town. In its heyday, it had sixteen to eighteen hotels, including several 'shanties'.

10,596 tons of ore was treated at Kalgoorlie, Boulder, Northam, and even outside the colony from 1 June 1898 to October 30. This ore was nearly all from the leads. The grand total of gold exported for those five months was determined to be 68,000 ounces, which would be valued at £340,000. The monthly output was at least £40,000 worth of gold. This was approximately a quarter of the gold yield of the whole colony. It was noted at this time however that the returns were petering out fast.

The *Sun* made the following report on the 9 July 1899, which I have included because of its humour:

"A Sharp Shooter Amok"

The inhabitants of this usually peaceful-even somnolent town were somewhat awakened last Tuesday owing to the foolhardy antics of an alluvialite who evidently possessed more lucre than cerebral tissue. Coming into town with a well-filled bag of "slugettes," one John James purchased a revolver at one of the local stores, asserting that he required it for the purpose of annihilating any future "ratters " of his camp. No sooner was the Colt given to him that he expressed a wish to try its capacities. The affrighted shopman immediately assumed the form of a monkey and crept out of the store.

ON ALL-FOURS.

One of the proprietors, however, stood his ground and managed to get rid of the disciple of Captain Carver with the loss of only a small portion of the roof. The self-constituted gen d'arme careered southwards, but after a few poor attempts at marksmanship near the Australia Hotel, our chief-in-blue appeared. After some amount of diplomacy, the boy desperado handed up his weapon and ammunition, and shortly after he was lodged in the local jug on a triple charge. Needless to say; he was duly punished for his stupid actions.

By 1902 the few graves in the old cemetery were hidden among piles of mullock left after the diggers had extracted their gold. The area became deserted, and rumours of 'strange haunting noises' and ghostly forms ensured the area became avoided at all costs, particularly after dark. However, there was one 'unbelieving' claim holder who lay in wait for these ghostly figures with a shotgun one night in 1903. He saw some figures in the night so fired. Fortunately, he missed, as he nearly shot the local bootmakers James and Billy Wyatt.

The two men were walking over the dumps searching for overlooked gold with a divining rod. They carried out their divining at night to avoid ridicule from their friends, as it was an unorthodox method. James's son bagged the promising patches of ore for treatment during daylight hours. One citizen said the enterprising man who solved the mystery of the ghostly figures should have been "presented with an illuminated address".

The following account by the reporter known as 'The Pelican' of the *Sun* on 28 June 1903, details how desperate Kanowna was becoming:

> Pugtown is passing through a period of unprecedented depression. The mines are closing down; the alluvial is becoming scarcer, and even beer is giving way to water. It is true, a melancholy-looking brewery driver still takes the beverage into town, but instead of piled-up barrels towering to a pyramid from the floor of the conveyance, a small and dejected keg now rides on its own to the abode of bung. When the driver, a tough-looking warrior with a bottlenose, had laboriously slid the pigmy cask down the skids

and planted it with a Herculean effort on the pub counter, he cast off a variety of remarks having reference to the dullness of trade. "The town is goin' tor the dorgs," he remarked with desperation. "Fancy comin' in all the way with that," pointing to the young cask he had just launched into position. "It's my belief we'll soon come down to one hogshead brews once a month if the blokes don't get a move on and consume more beer." "So bad as that," I inquired. "I should rather think it is," he replied, with aggravation in his voice. "Why we don't turn out enough grains to feed the horses". Swearing bitterly at the hardness of fate he scrambled aboard again and was soon a speck of dust in the dim perspective. That's how matters are in the beer line, and you may depend upon it when the fluid is not consumed in large quantities things are pretty blue. The Valley and Last Chance mines are closing up shop, and Shaker Mick is pulling down his gunya preparatory to flitting for fresh fields. It was the same way before the discovery of the North and Cemetery leads. Kanowna was comparatively deserted, and the field seemed doomed when the famous alluvial deposits were located, and once again prosperity set in. We want another revival badly to save us from drifting into utter obscurity (p7).

Unfortunately, another good find did not occur, and the town did finally die. The municipality dissolved in 1917. When war broke out in 1939, little remained of the once fine town of Kanowna. Only one hotel, school, hall, store, post office, a few houses and camps remained. The younger men gradually drifted away to enlist, then the school closed and the post office that once employed seven people was dismantled. The salvaged materials were used in the construction of buildings at the Parkeston Staging Camp. Kanowna's buildings were almost all sold and moved either to other goldfields towns or to the Wheatbelt (Bough).

A few prospectors with wives and families battled along for a while. The old-timers, too frail to seek new fields, fossicked over the old dumps and spent many hours yarning with each other about the "good old days" (Compton 16, 18).

The death of a town is a sad story, as it is really the death of a community. Of course, some feel the loss more keenly than others. I will end this account of Kanowna with a sad article published in the Perth *Daily News* on 17 January 1949:

> "Lonely Prospector Waiting to Die"
>
> In constant pain from the stump of an amputated leg, an 83-year-old bachelor dollies stone at his lonely tin camp in the ghost town of Kanowna while waiting to die.
>
> He is Irish-born Joe Palmer who has been prospecting for more than 50 years.
>
> "I have no friends and nowhere else to live," he said yesterday. "I don't like hospitals, cities or beer. All I want is to die."
>
> Although he is regarded locally as an uncommunicative hermit, he welcomes the occasional visitor with all the enthusiasm of a lonely man.
>
> When he interrupted his stay on the Goldfields to try coalmining his leg was cut off by a coal mining machine four days after he arrived at Collie. For 32 years his gold prospecting has been handicapped by an artificial leg and a partly crippled arm. He has never struck it rich, his best find being a 22oz slug which he picked up at Lake Darlot many years ago.
>
> Now when he uses his dollypot and pestle on odd stones he picks up he does not expect to find many colours. He is just "keeping out of the way and waiting to die".

And while waiting, he is avoiding all that is distasteful to him - the din of city life, raucous laughter and the tinkling of beer glasses.

Joe Palmer is one of Australia's loneliest men. His dolly pot is his only comfort.

The Wail of a Dryblower

I am a digger at Mulgabbie and I'd like to rise and say
Dryblowing is a swearfill game to most diggers anyway.
You work for days without a colour, then have a lengthy swear
that takes two solid windy days to cleanse the atmosphere.

If an angel down from heaven had to dryblow for a crust
got his aureola discoloured and his white wings red with dust
and panning off his prospect found he had not raised a grain
no doubt he'd proved a failure, but he'd try to be profane.

When you haven't a colour and your mouth is full of dust
and with dirt in you turned the colour of a terracotta bust
and your boots are full of pebbles, like a pilgrim to a shrine
then it is not for resignations, but for eloquence you pine

But you have your compensations if you barely make a crust
If of food your belly is empty, it is always full of dust.
If your luck is hard and rocky, let this thought your spirits cheer
you are opening up the country, you are a bally pioneer.

I guess the recording angel when he draws my balance sheet.
Will grin, and put my swear words down to the damper and tinned meat.
Hard luck, and flies, and dust, and things,
and say, things were rather tough,
and reckon that language had failed me and hadn't sworn enough.

I am full up of pioneering for my hat is full of holes,
and the upper of my boots are sadly parting from the soles,
For really it's no wonder that at times your spirits flag
when your pant's a piebald garment that is mended with bag.

The Wail of a Dryblower

So I am giving up prospecting, going give dryblowing best,
give my system and my swear words both a long much-needed rest.
going where there's decent tucker, tender steak and juicy chop.
Going where there's beer in plenty - and I am going to drink a drop

H. Galthrop,
Mulgabbie W.A
March 31, 1898

Chapter Four

Darlot: A Rush in the Wilderness

OF THE MANY GOLD RUSHES in the early days, the one farthest inland took place at Lake Darlot during 1895. Some brave men were pushing further inland from the Murchison and eastern goldfields, hoping to find their own El Dorado. Exploration in this direction called for experienced and tough men, as the country was dry with very few waterholes. Another danger came from the Aborigines, as they would often attack and spear these early explorers.

During 1894, some small parties discovered gold in the eastern areas that later became known as Lawlers. Soon after, three Englishmen named Parkes, Rogers, and Lockhart explored inland from Lawlers. They found gold near Lake Darlot, which is 140 kilometres north of Leonora.

Jim Cable, Bill McGennett, and Jack Pickering also found gold in the area. The new find was good, some parts of the field were strewn with

DARLOT: A RUSH IN THE WILDERNESS

easily seen pieces of gold. They named one area the Scorpion Patch.

These two groups decided there was enough gold in the area for everyone, so they joined forces to reduce the likelihood of potential attacks from Aboriginals. Their fear of attack was soon realised as Cable and Jennet were speared. Cable was speared in the groin.

Despite this, they concentrated on getting alluvial gold for several weeks. They then decided to return to Coolgardie as their supplies were getting low, Cable's wound was giving him trouble as the barb was still embedded, and he had also developed scurvy. They travelled 480 kilometres to get medical treatment in Coolgardie (*Western Mail*, [Perth], 16 Jan 1941, p9). They all agreed to keep the find a secret while in town.

Cable was later taken to Perth for more specialised attention, and Pickering went there for a holiday. While there, Pickering spent some of his new-found wealth in hotel bars. Despite his pledge to keep the find quiet, he was soon boasting of the wonderful gold find he had made. Cable was telling people he must have found Aladdin's Lamp.

Word was now out, and it travelled far and fast. Experienced men were soon on the trail. Prospectors flocked in from all directions - from the fields of Coolgardie and Menzies, as well as from the Murchison, Ashburton and Gascoyne Districts. Most went to Lawlers and carefully followed their tracks to the new find at Darlot. The traffic became so dense on this track that one disgusted pioneer said that it reminded him of "a walk down Bourke Street".

Within six weeks the population of the camp was between 3,000 to 4,000. The first to arrive on horseback pitched their tents by the long gully which carried the best gold. This area became known as Horseman's Gully. Others came with wagons or camel teams. The less fortunate came on foot with hand-carts carrying their outfits, pulling it like a horse with a yoke. Many pushed home-made wheelbarrows, and several walked, carrying their swags.

The wheels of the home-made wheelbarrows were made of softwood boards nailed together until they were around three inches thick and three feet high. Some had tin tyres, but mostly they were bare wood. The barrow was about six feet long with the wheel towards the centre. Most of the wheelbarrow men were middle-aged, and one observer said they could be classed as elderly.

The track was heavy, and some stages had over thirty miles between waters. The road from Coolgardie to Darlot, via Granite Creek, was nearly three-hundred miles. Long miles too, when the summer sun was blazing down (*Western Mail* [Perth], 16 Jan 1941, p9).

A newspaper reporter named W J Hamblin travelled to the rush on his pushbike from Coolgardie. It took him just under a fortnight to make the return journey. His report was published in the *Coolgardie Miner* on 7 May 1895. In it, he recommended not travelling to the rush on horses due to the long, dry stage. He also suggested taking enough provisions to last a few months. Most of the men were finding the climate trying, and many had contracted a fever. Several prospectors died from Typhoid, their grave sites are still visible today at Horseman's Gully.

A bicycle mail express service was soon inaugurated. These hardy souls reaped their own golden harvest by carrying letters and papers to and from Coolgardie at two-shillings and six-pence an article. Three to four hundred messages per trip were was the average (*West Australian* [Perth],18 July 1932, p16).

Heavy rain helped to solve the immediate problem of water, but it was a curse to the dryblowers. They lit fires on their muddy claims to hurry the drying process. However, the water problem at Darlot was soon overcome early by sinking a well into the subterranean basin that underlies these northern fields.

Most prospectors were lucky, as a high percentage of those early on the Darlot field obtained payable gold. There were no phenomenally rich claims or large nuggets, but while the gold lasted, there was "tucker at least for everyone". No reefs of value were discovered. One of the most promising was worked by Billy Frost, who was an outstanding explorer.

At first, provisions were scarce, and the food was costly. The first consignments were sold at public auction. The seller most likely had his own bidders in the audience, and prices went sky-high. The figure at which each article was sold then became the standard price. It was only at Klondyke in later years such exorbitant prices ruled again. They paid five pounds for a twenty-two-kilogram bag of flour, seven-shillings and six-pence to ten shillings for 450-grams of tea and one-pound five shillings for 450-grams of tobacco. These items were generally looked on as being the only absolute necessities. When a camel team arrived with a massive load of stores, the food situation improved. Before long, enterprising traders realised the opportunity for good profits and carted supplies to the miners on the field.

The auction sales remained a feature of early life at Darlot. On Saturday afternoons, mining requisitions and foodstuffs were often auctioned at very high prices.

Many fascinating characters were attracted to the Darlot rush, one being Moondyne Joe. Moondyn Joe (Joseph Bolitho Johns) is still infamous for his many innovative jailbreaks from Fremantle Prison. He was celebrated by Perth and Fremantle newspapers at the time.

Joe and his mate were both expert bushmen. They were on their way back to Nannine from the comparatively unexplored inland country of the Murchison. Their prospecting trip was mostly unsuccessful, so when they saw some smoke coming from the prospectors at Darlot, they saw an opportunity. They left after a few days as their supplies were low. They made the round trip to Nannine and were back in just three weeks. However, by this time, there were hundreds of drybowers at work and hundreds more arriving.

Few prospectors relied on dishes and sieves. Most of the prospecting parties had a dryblower, as they were considered the best gold-savers. Dryblowers came in all shapes and designs.

Some were rude contrivances formed by mulga sticks and old pieces of wire. One resident of the field described them as "looking as if they had been hewed out with a stone axe by some drunken and astigmatic-eyed cave dweller".

There were some fancy shakers made by a Coolgardie carpenter. The centrifugal dryblowing machines worked like large spinning tops that enabled a large amount of dirt to be put through, and they threw the gold out. Prospectors that used these were often called 'dish-twisters'.

There were also several of the bellows variety, the aristocrat of them being the Lorden. These were especially useful for fine gold on the flat above Horseman's Gully. The only negative side to them was that they were very heavy to move from place to place.

On Sundays, or when it rained, the dryblowers were forced to remain idle. Not being able to work, but able to gamble, hundreds of diggers would attend the two-up school. The ring-keeper was a well-known Victorian boxer. He ran the game fairly and kept order. The ring was immense, with the men who formed it not only placing their bets with the Spinner but also with each other. Hundreds of pounds changed hands at these games.

Considered the Napoleon among the gamesters was 'The Yank'. He was a bearded American who bet heavily. If he were temporarily cleaned out of money, he would throw into the ring his bulging chamois bag holding from 4,665 to 6,220 grams of gold. The crowd would then put up their money against the bag, knowing the weight claimed by the Yank would be correct. However, he rarely had to dip into the bag to pay out.

After two-up school finished, or after a successful day with the shaker, many diggers visited the numerous grog shanties. The largest of these was run by Charlie the Goose. His yarns and whisky at one-pound five-shillings a bottle was much appreciated after a hard, dusty day.

Charlie the Goose was originally from France and travelled most of the world as a soldier, sailor, showman and prospector. After Darlot, he went to Wiluna. Even with a severely injured leg, he always managed to get payable crushings from the state battery. He lived until he was well over ninety years of age (*The Magnet Mirror and Murchison Reflector* [Meekatharra], 30 September 1933, p1).

His mates put his home-made, wooden-wheeled barrow on his grave as a memento of his imperishable past. With all his belongings, he pushed this barrow from Cape York to Southern Cross and from there to Coolgardie. Another good, long push was from Dunns to Darlot and another from Hannans (Kalgoorlie) to Kurnalpi. He finally took the old wheelbarrow from Perth to Wiluna (*The Daily Telegraph* [Sydney],26 December 1933, p7).

Charlie had previously instigated a rush called the Goose's Puzzle. His mate, 'Pigweed Harry' told him of a good find north-east of Pindinni. They quickly put together ten horses, a cart, stores and supplies. Knowing this would attract the 'jackals' (men who follow the daring pioneers), they devised a plan to throw them off their scent. It had just rained, so their tracks were easy to follow. When they reached 'Boomerang Rock', which was a large sheet of granite, they dismantled their spring cart. They strapped everything, including the tanks and cart's wheels to their Brumbies. This worked, as the Jackals lost their tracks and returned to Coolgardie after a few days searching.

A few months later, Charlie and his mate arrived in town with two-hundred ounces of gold and staked a reward claim. His mate died a year later. Charlie never returned to his claim as he did not have much faith in other men. It became known as the Goose's Puzzle as no-one could work out how he hid his tracks, and he never revealed the location of the reward claim (*The Daily News,* [Perth], 30 September 1933, p11).

DARLOT: A RUSH IN THE WILDERNESS

One Christmas at Darlot, Bernie Liex's party decided to treat some other diggers to a Christmas dinner, as they had been quite successful at their dryblowing. The poultry and other fine foods were obtained from Leonora and the 'babbling brook' was commissioned to make the pudding. A guest recalled that:

> While preparing for the great event on Christmas morning, it was noticed that the sauce for the pudding had been overlooked. A meeting was immediately convened, and it was decided unanimously that the sauce must be brandy sauce, and Bernie was sent by horse post haste to the shanty for some brandy. He returned with a bottle, and the question arose as to what quantity of the brandy should be put into the sauce. After conferring for a

time, it was decided to put the whole contents of the bottle in.

Now, to relieve the monotony of camp life, it had been a practice to grant leave to one or other of the party on occasions to visit the district shanty, to pass judgment on the quality of the liquors, etc. Just before dinner one of them had returned from his "holiday," and his appetite was far from good. He was exhorted by all present to join in the festivities and partake of some of the poultry, but no good. On the arrival of the plum pudding and sauce he was remonstrated with by his mates for his unreasonable attitude, and after much bantering decided that, as it was Christmas time, he would try a little bit of pudding. A helping was given him, and at the first bite his hitherto dead eyes brightened considerably, and his spirits revived. "Have another piece of pudding," said the server. "Not much," was the reply, "but give me a bowl of the bloomin' sauce" (*Western Mail* [Perth], 20 May 1937 p11).

In 1897 there were three bush tragedies at Darlot.

The first death was Jack Tulloch who established the droving and butchering firm of Tulloch & Co with Jim Willis. He perished near Abercrombie on the Lawlers-Wiluna Road while moving sheep. There was little water around, and he got severely dehydrated. Unable to continue, he sent his Aboriginal assistant to Lawlers to get help. By the time the assistant returned with others to help him, he had perished. He was buried where he died, and his mates put up a headstone. His grave became another lonely grave in the goldfields.

The second tragedy was the murder of Henry Reason by local Aborigines. He was murdered at a watering place called Wingarra Mire, near Mistake Creek. Reason left Darlot in February, and his body was found just before Easter. The men who found the body were Hubert O'Grady, Clarrie Brown, a New Zealander called Hickey and an Aboriginal boy. They arrived at Wingarra Mire about mid-day and decided to give the camels a day's spell. After they had lunch, they all rested in the shade, except for the boy. He went looking around the bush and returned a little- later. He told the others, "I think the blacks been kill someone here."

Reason's camel, saddles, and gear were burnt. O'Grady found the body some distance away under some bushes. Mounted Constable Breen arrested several Aboriginals, and they were taken to the police station in Lawlers. They escaped from custody and were not recaptured.

It was said that Reason's death was somewhat his own fault. Before anything was known of the murder, the Aboriginals who were arrested came to Darlot. One of them was being carried by his mates as he had an injured foot. It was believed they were trying Reason's revolver and it went off, the bullet going through his foot.

The third tragedy was the death by dehydration of a father and son named Luke, some eighteen or twenty miles from Darlot. The remains were not found until the spring of 1898. Two stray horses came into Darlot in October 1897, and it was likely theirs. It was surmised that their horses got away from them and they perished when they were following them.

Arthur Ashwin and his mates went prospecting in the spring of 1899, and found the remains of the father. A few weeks later, Aboriginals at the British King mine reported that they had found the bones of a child. The remains were found a distance apart. The Aboriginals advised the authorities that they saw the body of the father soon after his death but did not report it, as they were concerned they might be accused of murdering him (*Western Mail*, [Perth] 6 May 1937, p11) (*Inquirer and Commercial News*, Perth, 24 Dec 1897).

When the township was gazetted on Jan 14 1898, it was called Woodarra. This is the Aboriginal name given to the adjacent granite rocks from which the town's water supply came.

The government battery was opened on 19 February 1898 and employed nine men. Over 1,000 tons of ore were crushed from March to October that year, for an average yield of 1.75 ounces per ton. The State Government purchased the Darlot battery in 1901 and relocated it to the Ballangarry mine. Over the next eight years, over fifteen-million tonnes of ore were milled for a return of over 25,000 ounces of gold – the highest of any State Battery in WA at the time (Bell Sally and Eaton).

In 1899, a butcher who was camped out of town in a tent was visited by Aboriginals. They showed him a nugget weighing approximately seven ounces that they found near his tent. They were happy to swap it for a fifty-pound bag of flour (*The Mount Leonora Miner*, 15 July 1899, p3).

Businesses in the town in 1899 included three stores owned by W M Beale, Haley, and the Metzke Brothers. W Pearce was the butcher and J L Simon the baker. The first hotel, the Dew Drop Inn was opened in 1896. The Coolgardie Miner stated that it was appropriately named, as like the old ballad, "the roof lets in the sunshine and the rain, and if the dew comes, it will let that in too". The Ballingarry and the Woodarra Hotel opened soon after (Sharp).

The Darlot Progress Committee had been lobbying the Government for some time to improve water conditions. In March 1903, a water boring plant finally arrived. The townsfolk were disappointed to find it was a little older than expected. A rumour started that the plant was brought to Australia by Captain Cook – and they thought that by its appearance, this may well be true! (Bell Sally and Eaton)

The following report on Darlot was made in *the Mount Leonora Miner* on 18 April 1903 (p2):

> A correspondent, who claims that Darlot is receiving but scant recognition from the Government, supplies the Press with the following: — During the past twelve months no less than 16 parcels have been treated from different reefs, and only in three instances has the return been below one ounce per ton, and the highest was 54oz.
>
> The St. George is located in the centre of the old alluvial ground. It is owned by Messrs Metzke Bros., W. Hurst and party, and consists of 12 acres. During the past ten months, 225 tons have been milled, for 5,750oz. of smelted gold, worth £3 18s 6d per ounce. Up to the present time the reef has not been tapped below water level, a depth of 90ft. Splendid gold is showing underfoot. Expert opinion estimates the present chute to be worth 60,000oz.
>
> The Waikato is located two miles in a southwesterly direction from the St. George and is owned by Mr J. Metzke. Since its discovery, 800 tons have been treated, giving a return of 1,140oz., valued at £3 12s 6d per ounce. The chute is proved for 320ft. The deepest shaft is 38ft. The owner is demonstrating his faith in the property by erecting a pumping plant and when it is complete 12 men will be employed. Mr Metzke anticipates being in full swing in six weeks' time and will break 100 tons of stone per month, at an estimated value of 30dwts per ton.

The Filbandint, the Zambar, and the Monte Christo consist each of twelve acres running in a north-westerly direction and is the one line of reef. The Filbandint, out the south-east end, was opened up about nine months ago by Trinidad Bros. One hundred and seven tons taken from the reef average-8ft wide gave the owners the handsome return of 272oz. At present, the owners are sinking. There is every indication of the property opening up well.

On the north-western end is the Zambar, owned and worked by Messrs Tom, Kerr and party. A small test parcel of 18 tons, taken from wall to wall of a 10ft reef, gave a return of 6dwt. 14gr per ton. Under present conditions, this is not payable, and so far not much development work has been done. A portion of the reef is being taken from one wall, which should return over an ounce per ton.

North-west again, the Monte Christo is located. It is owned partly by an old and tried prospector, best known as Black Christie. Ninety tons are now in the process of treatment at the State battery, and 25dwt per ton is a low estimate of its worth. The reef is open to a depth of 40ft., showing a face of 12ft., 4ft wide. The parcel under treatment being a distance of five miles from the battery, taking it from wall to wall would probably not pay, while, with a battery on the ground I have no hesitation in stating that this line of reef would be among the highest dividend payers in Western Australia.

King of the Hills is owned by Messrs. Aitken Bros. Twenty-four tons treated last month gave the owners 28oz of smelted gold. The deepest level is 90ft. Good stone is being broken at the present time.

The Rise and Shine belongs to Messrs Swanson and McGuire. Twelve months ago a pocket of over 50oz. of dollying stone was unearthed. Since then nothing of importance has been discovered, though the owners are still sanguine.

The East End of the property of Messrs Metzke Bros. Forty tons treated five months ago returned 122oz. Stone equally rich is being raised at the present time.

The Morning Light is being worked on tribute by Messrs Miller and Fisher. A shaft has been sunk to a depth of 100ft. The firm is now cross-cutting to tap the reef. Horseworks are used for hauling purposes. Up to 5oz per ton has been taken from this property. The reef, though small, is rich.

The Ballingarry has had over 1,000 tons milled at the State battery during the latter part of last year, averaging 11dwts per ton. The reef is from 4ft to 6ft wide. The mine is at present under exemption. Work will shortly be resumed by the owners Messrs Smith and Dunstall.

From the Balmoral 22 tons of stone were treated, giving a return 22oz. 6dwt. This lease is abandoned though well worth a trial.

The Amazon, which is one of the most consistent properties in the district, is owned and worked by Messrs Skinner and Paterson. Over 1,100 tons of stone have been taken from this mine. During the past nine months, 320 tons treated locally returned 1,900oz. Six men are at present raising stone. Two hundred tons have been raised and will be treated shortly. Several other parties are at work on payable stone, but space will not permit me referring to them in this report.

One word regarding the pastoral industry. During the past two years, 200,000 acres of grazing land has been taken up by local residents, who have at present over 700 head of cattle depasturing within a radius of 20 miles of Darlot. This bids fair to become an important industry and needs encouraging.

The population of our district is estimated at 175 adults. The town consists of two hotels, one store, a hairdresser's establishment, fruiterer, and newsagent and blacksmiths' shops, and we trust ere long to be able to add post and telegraph offices. Our local progress committee will not rest content until this is an accomplished fact.

The towns of Darlot and Lawlers had many sporting competitions. The first of many annual cricket matches were played between the two communities in 1897. These grew into week-long affairs held twice a year. They also had shooting competitions, and a tennis court brought further inter-field competition and social occasions. Banquets and balls were planned around these events. In 1908, the Lake Darlot Race Club was formed under WA Turf Club rules. The last entry in the Club's cash book was April 1929.

As the various claims ran out of gold, their owners drifted away. The Mount Black rush practically depopulated Darlot. This rush turned out to be a rumour or a hoax, but many decided to return to more settled fields. From the outbreak of World War One until the 1950's there was very little mining activity in the region.

By 1930, both the hotels had closed. The proprietors of Watsons store were the last residents in the area. They finally left in 1952. Eventually, all that remained was the cemetery and the ruins of the battery.

With regards to Darlot's modern history, interest in the area resumed again in the mid-1980's. A new treatment plant was moved from Mt Fisher in 1988. Sundowner Minerals estimated achieving a yield of 73,000 ounces of gold from the leases they acquired.

Ownership of the operations changed hands four times in nine years.

Darlot: A Rush in the Wilderness

By 1994, Darlot was an open-pit mine 1.3 kilometres long and 120 metres deep. Open pit mining ceased in 1995 in favour of underground mining. The Centenary deposit was discovered in 1996. In October 2017, Red5 acquired the operation as a going concern.

Unlike the old days, there is no townsite. Now there is a mining camp with 204 rooms, a mess and other camp facilities for 'fly-in, fly-out' workers (Red5 Limited) (Bell Sally and Eaton).

Darlot (For Dad)

Drifting through the desert mulga
Reaching into crystal skies
Soft as birdsong in the dawning
Do you hear the spirits calling?

Come – Return once more
And make your camp
For here we hold your captive heart –
Here – In Fishers wide embrace.

And well we know this country,
You and I
Each jutting outcrop and campsite thicket
Her saltbush flats and ironstone ridges
Look there – a single fragile flower!
And there – The distant breakaways
On a blue horizon sweep

Darlot – Ancient land of Blackman dreaming
Timeless and Peaceful
Bejewelled landscape
Yours to share-
by day – sun warmed nuggets of molten gold
by night – a diamond swag of stars.

Ainslea Devine

(Sharp)

Chapter Five

The Cycle Specials of Coolgardie

THE POEM BELOW APPEARED IN *Cycling News* in 1899. The story of the specials officially begun in Coolgardie in April 1894, with the formation of the Coolgardie Cycle Express Company.

Cycling in the West

The specials ride for a bob a mile
And they earn it every bean
They cover the shadeless plains in style
That would may you East men green

For if ever a man deserved his pay
It's the cyclist who can pass
A hundred miles in a ten-hour day
On a cover stuffed with grass …

The Cycle Specials of Coolgardie

There's none of your billiard-table tracks
To the soaks, where the specials train.
There's the glint of the dread 'three-cornered jacks'
And the thick red dusty plain.

There's the 'double-jees' on the iron-stone rise.
There's the stump and the hidden hole
Where the shriek of the puncture signifies
The song of the cyclist's soul.

They carry their lives in their midget kits,
Who pace on the golden trails,
And they grovel down in their hand-scraped pits
When the willy-willy wails.

With the midget lost and the tyre cut through
And the waterbag run dry,
The special turns to the East he knew
And spreads the sand to die.

An article in the *Coolgardie Miner* of 21 April read:

> Well-known crack Victorian cyclists establish a cycling telegraph. Five shillings for messages to Southern Cross. Services also to Hannan (Kalgoorlie), White Feather (Kanowna) and Kurnalpi. It was originated by Summerhayes and Bamlett. Money for the cyclists' express raised by one hundred and twenty-five shares of £2 each."

The service was an important one. The railway had not yet reached the goldfields, and the bicycle was the fastest and most economical means of providing a courier or mail service. Many of the independent cyclists providing similar services joined the company.

The company had a postcard printed and distributed copies to potential customers, below is a reproduction:

> **THE**
> **Coolgardie Cycle Express Co.**
> HUNT STREET,
> (*Opposite Post Office*)
>
> **SPECIAL CYCLE MESSAGES.**
>
> HAVING engaged the services of the following Special Cyclists:— F. P. HOPE, H. YEATES, F. W. WILSON, F. W. BROOKMAN, W.H. HAMBLIN, J. H. C. BAMLETT, &c., we are prepared to convey messages to any part of the Field, by day or night, at shortest notice.
>
> Mining Notices put up on Claims, Wages Paid, Claims Pegged and taken up at Warden's Office, and all Mining Business transacted.
>
> *Regular Cycle Mail leaves this office for Hannans, (daily) Menzies, Niagara, Yerilla, Pindinni, Mt. Margaret, Norseman, Dundas, &c.*
>
> **JAMES A. HEALY, AGENT.**
> N.B.—SPECIAL MESSAGES GUARANTEED.

(Sheriff")

At first, all letters sent from the service were stamped with the word 'Paid'. Agent Healy later got George Vinden, the printer from the Coolgardie Miner, to produce the company's own stamps. These course blue stamps, as shown below, could be purchased in Healy's office in Coolgardie or their agents located in the mining centres. Authorised postage stamps were added if the mail collected at these places were destined for towns farther on from Coolgardie.

The Cycle Specials of Coolgardie

In 1895, stamps depicting camels were printed. These were used on mail intended for outlying districts where camels proved to be more economical than bicycles. The camel stamps were used for only six months. By December 1896, the postal authorities claimed Healy's services were infringing the postal monopoly, so they forced him to close. By this time, Cobb & Co. Royal Mail coaches had extended their services to take mail and passengers to most parts of the goldfields.

Despite the ban, another stamp was printed for special cyclists. H Lacye-Hillier and F E Maskell's service began in late 1896. They only operated between Coolgardie and Lake Lefroy. Lake Lefroy is near Widgiemooltha.

At this time, the district had a population increase of some three-hundred men. This was because Sam Pearce pegged out twenty blocks and bought a little mine in the area called the Lady of the Lake for the Brookman Syndicate. They employed men to develop the mine and leases. This attracted other prospectors to the area. However, this only lasted a few months as the syndicate failed to uncover any new rich discoveries.

In February 1897, the stamp below was printed, but the service and

The Cycle Specials of Coolgardie

the stamps only lasted six months. They received a letter from Mr Scholl, the Post Master of Western Australia, advising them that the stamp infringed postal regulations. They had to cease their service to avoid being prosecuted.

As these stamps are now so rare and collectable, the pair pictured above sold at auction in 2004 for $21,275!

The special cyclists had a difficult job travelling through the uninhabited bush in extreme weather conditions. They also had breakdowns to contend with, and in some districts, particularly around Darlot, they had hostile Aborigines that might attack them.

If the Cycle Express men became aware of a cable sitting in the telegraph office at Coolgardie that contained an offer for a mine, the good news of flotation in London, or a similar message, on their own responsibility they would deliver the cable. Sometimes they got nothing if the coded cable showed the float to be a failure, but some received fifty-pounds to one-hundred pounds for good news. Once a cyclist who travelled seventy-miles miles to deliver good news, got a parcel of original paid-up scrip that eventually paid £750.

The founder of the Cycle Express in Coolgardie, Joe Bamlett, had a reputation for getting mail through whatever the conditions were.

In 1894 he was cycling between Coolgardie and Dundas, close to the Forty Mile Rocks, when he heard an unusual noise behind him. Unable to identify the sound, he stopped peddling and looked around. A pack of dingoes was bearing down on him, he could hardly believe his eyes!

He wasted no further time in thought and quickly got back on his bike – the race was on! The road was smooth, but he had great difficulty in keeping a distance between himself and the dingo pack. At times they came uncomfortably close, one snapped at him and nearly pulled him off his bike. Bamletts's strong legs kept up their work, and he just managed to keep ahead of them.

At one point he got some 250 yards ahead of them. As he knew soft uphill country lay just ahead, he stopped and threw his new nickel-plated spanner at them and they stopped for a short time. Several kilometres later he reached the end of Lake Cowan.

The lake was dry and hard as there had been no rain for some time. His wheels sped over the smooth surface at a 'terrific rate', and at last he could outdistance the pursuers. One after another the dingoes gradually fell behind. Bamlett finished the final thirty-two kilometres by moonlight without incident. He had never been so glad to reach an overnight stopping place (*Sunday Times* [Perth], 26 February 1922, p4).

A week earlier another cyclist had to shoot the leader of the pack to escape them.

The following poem about the incident was published in the

The Cycle Specials of Coolgardie

Coolgardie Miner (27 October 1894, p3):

> Dear Bamlett your story so truthful and plain,
> Will bring you more fame than a Bayley's:
> The yarn has been flashed far over the main
> To appear in the T'other-side dailies.
>
> 'Twill frighten the parents whose sons have come here,
> The glittering pennyweight seeking.
> And brothers and sisters will mingle a tear
> With sweetheart's hysterical shrieking.
>
> They'll picture their darlings aroused in the night,
> To fight like the heroes in dramas.
> And they'll shudder to think that the moon's misty light
> Will shine on their empty pyjamas.
>
> You told how they hungrily raced for your gore.
> No detail you skipped or omitted,
> And the snapping of fangs and the sickening roar,
> That rang in your ears as you flitted.
>
> Did you start when the howling first fell on your ears
> Like the voices of demons infernal?
> Why, it reads like a story that sometimes appears
> In the novels and Young Ladies Journal.
>
> Some cynics declare you've been studying Burns,
> And your race was a fake and a schlanter.
> I've heard them say Bammlet assuredly yearns
> To pose as a "Tammas O'Shanter."

The Cycle Specials of Coolgardie

> And others are making a paltry attack
> On the story I know to be truthful
> By saving the whisky you use on the track
> Carries forty-four snakes to the toothful.
>
> They know very well that spirits you keep
> For mending your tyre pneumatic,
> And as on the ground you've sometimes to sleep,
> To keep off the cramps and rheumatic.
>
> When the Light Brigade charge no more has a place,
> And Trafalgar has died from our lingo,
> Still shall live in our annals that bicycle race
> When Bamlett defeated the dingo

Bamlett eventually ended up in Gosnells growing oranges, lemons and other fruit (*Sunday Times* [Perth], 22 March 1931, p7).

Walter Hamblin was another exceptional rider. His is notable for having taken the first mail through from Coolgardie to Lake Darlot. This route is 320km of particularly rough country. He also rode the 960km route between Coolgardie and Cue. This seven-day marathon was also a 'first'.

The December 1896 issue of the *Australian Cyclist* featured a story about Hamblin and two other cyclists, Underwood and Grant. This story was not about their mail-carrying but about their journey to a new find at Mount Black, Mount Black is four-hundred kilometres north-east of Coolgardie.

They departed from Coolgardie camped at Cattle Swamp after riding ninety-six kilometres the first day. After breakfasting on 'tin dog' and damper, they worked on the best route to take. Being the most experienced bushmen, Hamblin and Underwood decided they should travel via Mount Margaret. As the first water supply was only forty kilometres away at a granite rock with gnamma holes, they decided not to carry water. This was a surprising decision for experienced bushmen to make as it was summertime.

Unfortunately, 170 tonnes of mining machinery had been hauled over the track sometime before their departure. The first eight kilometres of the track was in a fair condition, but the subsequent sandy stretches had been cut up severely by the heavy, horse-drawn wagons. It took them twenty minutes of strenuous effort to travel just one kilometre. By noon the temperature was forty-three degrees Celsius, and the men were becoming dehydrated.

Grant could not continue, so his more hardened companions left him lying in the shade of a bush. They carried on, aiming to reach the precious water and return with some for Grant.

At 4pm they came across a hopelessly bogged wagon-load of machinery. Fortunately, the teamsters had left behind a water bag containing two litres of water. The two men had a drink, and Hamblin was about to return to his friend with the remaining water when some camel men appeared. They offered to take the water to Grant.

For some reason, the camel men did not reach Grant. When Hamblin and Underwood had rested for a while, they rode back to see why Grant had not caught up with them. They found him in a bad state. He was so desperate with thirst he had drunk the oil from his cycle lamp. This caused him to have violent bouts of vomiting. Hamblin left him in the care of Underwood while he rode on to the rocks to get water.

On the way to the rocks, Hamblin met a prospector called Jim Caulfield who gave him some of his little water supply. Hamblin returned to his partners with the water, which was just sufficient to enable Grant to ride with them to the rocks and gnamma holes.

When they finally arrived at the precious gnamma holes, they found some prospectors camped nearby. The prospectors gave them some flour, and they cooked some Johnny cakes. Hamblin and Underwood ate hungrily, but Grant was still too weak and sick to eat.

The next morning the trio set off for Donkey Rocks, which was sixty-four kilometres away. By the time they reached their destination, Grant was in a 'fainting condition' and too ill to continue. Fortunately, some Teamsters agreed to take Grant with them to the Ninety Mile (Goongarrie). Hamblin and Underwood were now free to continue their journey and search for the new gold find.

They left Donkey Rocks with only four-and-a-half litres of water and a few potatoes. Their bad luck continued, as the hot sand caused Underwood's back inner-tube to burst. They had great difficulty in trying to find a way to hold it together in the heat. By 11am the next day, they had reached the little mining settlement of Pindinni.

Here they replenished their supplies and travelled the final fifty kilometres of the road to Mount Margaret. They then set off into unchartered sand and spinifex country in search of the supposed Mount Black gold find. For two days they searched, but they saw no sign of human life, let alone a gold rush. They had to return to Mount Margaret before their supplies and water ran out.

The Cycle Specials of Coolgardie

Three weeks from the day of departure, they rode back into Coolgardie with no shoes, as they had been worn out. Their rat-trap pedals were bound with sheepskin to protect their bare feet from the sharp teeth. Their shirts and trousers were torn and ragged. The whole ordeal had been for no purpose, as the mythical Mount Black has not been discovered till this day.

The specials continued to deliver messages after they were forced to stop carrying mail. At the Feysville and Block 48 rushes on the Hampton Plains in 1898, a cyclist went daily from Kalgoorlie to deliver copies of the *Kalgoorlie Miner* newspaper. The *Sunday Sun* reported:

> The daily Kalgoorlie papers are delivered from camp to camp by that champion bicyclist of the Westralian roads, Mr J Bigwood, who, miraculous as it may appear, rides the thirty-seven miles out and back each day with perfect punctuality, delivering his heavy load as he goes and thereby probably raising his daily little tour to something link eighty miles a day over one of the worst roads in the colony.

Several old specials became involved in competitive sports. Cycle racing had become one of the major sports on the eastern goldfields by the turn of the century. Coolgardie's famous yearly Westral Wheel Race attracted riders from all over Australia and overseas. Instead of pedalling through kilometres of the lonely bush with only the odd kangaroo or emu to see them pass, the ex-cycle specials were watched by crowds of cheering and enthusiastic onlookers and punters.

The Cycle Specials of Coolgardie

The only reminder we now have of these incredible athletes are a few, very collectable stamps and advertising cards in collectors' catalogues.

Reference photo from WA Historical Cycling Club website: http://historicalcycleclub.com.au/events/2014/6/30/talk-by-author-jim-fitzpatrick

Chapter Six

The Not So Modest Smiler Hales

THE EARLY DAYS OF THE eastern goldfields had quality local newspapers. By the end of 1895, Coolgardie had seven newspapers. The *Coolgardie Miner* and the *Chronicle* published each morning and the *Golden Age* each evening. The *Mining Review Courier,* the *Mining Review* and the short-lived *'Othersider* were weekly publications.

One of the most colourful journalists in Coolgardie at that time was Alfred G 'Smiler' Hales. In June 1894, he was an editor, sub-editor, chief of staff, and principal contributor editor of the Coolgardie Miner. He "provided the Old Camp with some lively reading even for those lively times" (*Western Mail* [Perth], 20 May 1937).

One day when he was a free-lance journalist for the *Courier,* he went out on his brumby to Hannan's Find and other mines around Kalgoorlie. He visited Brown Hill, which was just about to be floated in London. Captain Treloar and Bob Pettigrew owned the lease and they promised Smiler one-hundred shares.

Hales wrote a glowing report on the property which ran into about four inches of printed matter, around sixty lines. A few months later the stock market increased dramatically, so Smiler rushed to Howard Taylor's share depot and sold his shares for six-hundred pounds – equal to ten pounds per line! Therefore, he was probably the highest paid journalist of the time (Spinifex, "Rise and Fall of Journalism in the

Old Camp", *Western Mail* [Perth], 21 July 1907, p1).

Reproduction of illustration in "A. G. Hales – Miner and Journalist", *Referee* [Sydney], 23 December 1891, p6

He often liked to write in a biblical style. His first editorial, or 'Coolgardie Tailings', was written in this fashion:

What I have seen in Coolgardie? Verily as my soul liveth the place teems with sights that are strange and ways that are wonderful. I have been dragged into quiet corners, and mine ears have been filled with stories concerning great gold finds. Some of these tales were true, but alas some I knew were as false as the inside of hell ... A Coolgardie mining liar is one of the most stupendous works of nature.

He published a book of proverbs and 'sinful sermons'. One of his proverbs advised: "If a lady tells you her breasts are all her own, believe her, for it is better to be deceived than to be caught by her husband feeling for the naked truth". Among his sinful sermons was one about the convicts who were brought out to Western Australia from England between 1850 and 1863:

Now it came to pass in the days when the West land was young that most of the white tribes who inhabited this country dwelt by the seashore. A goodly number of them lived in one high dwelling which they termed in the vernacular of the times 'the jug', and they had many servants to wait upon them to see that they went to bed early and did not sleep too long in the morning ... Some of these servants wore red coats and carried a gun with a bayonet in the end thereof to keep the tribes from wandering too far from home and peradventure from also jumping their neighbour's landmark or anything else that was jumpable for that matter. Some of the other servants of these peculiar tribes wore blue raiment with yellow buttons, and it was part of their duty to see that the clothes of the tribesmen filled them ...They also had peculiar ornaments made unto like bullock chains with a ball attached which they fastened every morning to the legs of these strange men to remind them that it was not lawful to try and climb over a neighbour's landmark ...

The servants used to allow these people to amuse themselves hunting for sandalwood or in hewing timber or in making roads.

> They did good or evil as seemed well in their eyes and many of them were gathered to their fathers and were buried beneath the marble slab or a slab of mud but mud or marble it made devilish little difference to the worms under the soil, a fact which many of you will do good to remember for you in your turn will be gathered in by the Great Reaper and when you are six feet underground you won't count a cent more than the human that is buried along-side of you.

The unexpected sight of a lady barber in Coolgardie delighted and brought out a romantic streak in him:

> Fancy coming all the way into this abode of desolation, this land of whisky and wildcat schemes, and thus lighting on a spot where one could get shaved by a woman with a face like a spring poet's dream and a figure that instinctively brought back memories of my first waltz by moonlight. I'm going there to be shaved regularly, whether the boss carries a gun or not.

Although he did not approve of further numbers of Afghans entering Coolgardie, he described those already there as "dark-skinned men dressed in voluminous pantaloons of snowy white and jackets of fantastic fashion while their heads are surmounted by turbans coiled gracefully around brows that are not devoid of intelligence."

He was very severe on the alleged mining experts. He wrote: "Fathers of families, I say unto you, if you have a son who hath a genius for lying, reprove him not; he hath a glorious future in front of him as a mining expert" (*Table Talk*, [Melbourne], 11 April 1901).

The Coolgardie newspapers only lasted while the town prospered. When Hannans (Kalgoorlie) began booming, some of the newspaper men and their printing presses moved there. Before the turn of the century the *Western Argus,* the *Kalgoorlie Miner,* the *Sunday Sun* and the *Boulder Star* were all being printed in Kalgoorlie and Boulder.

Hales edited the evening paper, the *Boulder Star*, during its short life. When it ceased publication in 1899, he ran a half licence pub on the outskirts of the 'Old Camp'. It had a boxing stadium at the back. Mick Dooley was the boxing instructor and Hales often had the mitts on. According to a local report, he was only taking lessons, even though he was handy with his fists.

The Premier, Sir John Forrest, stopped at Kalgoorlie for a few hours in March 1899 while on route to Menzies. He was going there to open the new railway line. At the time, many miners in Kalgoorlie and Boulder were angry about a new mining law on alluvial rights that had resulted in the arrest of several defiant miners. He was surprised to see the whole area from the railway station to the Railway Hotel packed with miners. They were hoping he would address them from the balcony of the hotel. When he failed to do so, they became disappointed and angry. As the official party walked back to the train, an umbrella carried by his secretary accidentally hit him in the ribs when they were jostled by the crowd. The incident was greatly magnified, particularly in Eastern State's newspapers. Hales had been in Kalgoorlie at the time and wrote his version of the event for the *Daily Mail:*

> I saw Sir John standing alone amidst ten thousand diggers all seething with wrath. I saw that mighty mob of bearded men surge around him, saw the troopers vainly attempting to get to him to protect him. With a few words, Forrest could have changed their blind wrath to tumultuous cheering, but he would not utter the

words because he had been threatened. A man in the front rank struck him in the face. He bounded forward and dashed his fist into the face of his assailant. The mob swayed to and fro, growling wrathfully. He did not flinch. Flushed, lonely but game he faced the wild throng. Then a voice rolled over the crowd, "By God, he's game". Thousands of bare arms waved in the air. Thousands of voices game him cheer.

An unimpressed journalist from the *Sunday Sun* drily commented: "And thus history is made but fancy Oom John bounding forward if you can". Sir John Forrest was very portly.

The weekly *Sunday Sun* asked Hales to be their war correspondent in the Boer War. He didn't have enough money for the fair over, so the hat was passed around. At the head of the subscription list was A E Morgans, even though he "had experienced more of the rough side of Smiler's pen and tongue than any other goldfielder" ("Smiler Hales', *Western Mail* [Perth], 20 May 1937, p11).

Hales travelled with the Western Australian contingent that left Albany for South Africa in November 1899. He had heard that there was a shortage of fodder for horses in the Transvaal so decided to take a bicycle with him. Mr P. Armstrong, who sold bikes in Hannan Street, heard of Smiler's intention and gifted him a new road racer. We do not know if Hales ever followed his horse-mounted companions to battle on his bicycle, but a cable received in February 1900, reported his capture by the Boers due to falling off a horse.

He was only their prisoner for a month, as he was released in exchange for a Boer prisoner. He conscientiously sent his reports back to the *Sunday Sun*. A rival Coolgardie newspaper admitted that his descriptions of the Magersfontein battle were the 'brightest and best printed in Australia'.

Hales accused other war correspondents of great exaggeration:

> Four or five thousand mounted Boers were seen by our scouts in the direction of Jacobsvaal, the nearest Boer town in the Orange Free State, but they promptly bolted as soon as our advance lines came into sight, without firing a shot. The next day our fellows were in camp as usual singing hymns and playing pitch and toss. We had simply marched up a hill and marched down again, but the Sedlitz powder mind of the Capetown journalist fairly fizzed over the event and columns of hogwash concerning Australian smartness filled the papers. They praised our horsemanship, our shooting, our marching prowess, and everything from our boots to our heads. God knows what for. I don't …

It was not long before several of the Eastern States' newspapers were copying Smiler Hales' Boer War stories. The *Sunday Sun* lost their correspondent to the *London Daily Mail*. For the next twenty-odd years Hales was a correspondent at most armed battles, including the war in the Balkans and the Russo-Japanese war.

Hales was apparently willing to go undercover for a good story. This account was published in the *Barrier Miner* [Broken Hill] on 24 September 1903:

> "SMILER" HALES (writes a contributor in a contemporary) now wears a frock coat and a bell-topper and is said to change his collar daily. My first introduction to Smiler was one dusty day many years ago when he was riding furiously a big chestnut horse up and down Argent-street, Broken Hill. Someone said: "That flash bloke is mining reporter for THE BARRIER MINER" Hales

The Not-So-Modest Smiler Hales

nearly ran over me, and we had a drink at Mrs Oliver's, in Oxide-street, then the leading hostelry. In those days Hales wore corded breeches and his boots outside, also an Oxford shirt, a canvas coat, and a cabbage-tree hat. Soon after that date he disguised himself and got into the Junction mine, which was keeping its show dark. THE BARRIER MINER made a splash over his report. Hales bombarded the Bulletin for years with his photographs, in disguise and out of it, but Archibald gave him no advertisement. Afterwards, and because of his exploit, he fought a mine manager with his bares in the managerial dining-room. There were only about 20 persons present, and Hales had to acknowledge himself fairly beaten. Boxing boomed then on the Barrier, and Hale's vivid account of it won him a similar post on a Sydney paper.

Smiler Hales led a very full life over the next thirty years. As well as working as a journalist and war correspondent he gave many lectures, wrote fifty novels and even a play.

In 1931 a friendly acquaintance of his reported in the *Labour Call* ([Melbourne], 2 September 1931, p2):

> Last time I saw him, he was bubbling over with a prospective fortune in a play he had written. It was this play that led him to advertise in the London press: "I have the best drama since The Silver King. I want it read by somebody with money, enterprise and intelligence. The tin gods of the stage are unapproachable, save through their underlings, who have sawdust where brains should be. There is £10.000 in this drama."

In 1901 he wrote an article "All about myself" for a London Publication:

> Tell you something about my life; well, what is there to tell? ' I wrote a book- called 'The Wanderings of a Simple Child.' It had a

big sale in Australia. I furnished a house in gorgeous style on the time-payment system on the strength of it, but I had an unsatisfactory agreement with the publisher, and in the end the bailiff slept more often on the couch than I did; so I left it, to him. I have written more stories than I have hair on my head, and I am not bald yet. I have owned newspapers, gold mines, silver, mines, opal mines, and racehorses, and kept poor on the lot. Someday, if I am lucky, I hope to own a hen farm and be happy. ... I have been in a lot of places, and have seen a lot of people, the most honest, civil, and intelligent of whom is the London policeman; the most skilful and unscrupulous, the London cabman, I don't think much of missionaries, politicians, soldiers, authors or actors. The best fellows I have ever met are hard-up, hard-working, gritty newspaper fellows; the worst are successful writers suffering from 'swelled head. Why did I go to the African War, eh? — To get fame? Not a bit of it; I went hoping to get a bullet so that I might dodge the workhouse in my old age" (*The Toscin,* [Melbourne], 3 October 1901, p3).

When he was seventy-one, he wrote *Broken Trails,* a book recording his personal experiences. The autobiography claimed that it was he who first suggested the formation of League of Nations. A book reviewer said that the *Broken Trails* was written by one 'who has always realised the truth of the German proverb that modesty is an ornament, yet people get on better without it'. Perhaps the reviewer was right, in a chapter addressed to Australia, Smiler said:

Can you name me half a dozen men who had ever cut a figure in the world of men? Not one woman, with the possible exception of Madam Melba. Of the men, I can only visualise one. And modesty, by besetting sin, forbids me to name him. You may not agree with this but posterity will. A man who can write and publish fifty novels and at the same time leave his foot trails over

The Not-So-Modest Smiler Hales

four-fifths of the globe can't be blown aside like last year's leaves.

Reproduction of an ink drawing of Smiler Hales, https://trove.nla.gov.au/work/219994723

The Not-So-Modest Smiler Hales

Chapter Seven

'Roll-up': The Law of the Diggers

UNLIKE THE WILD WEST of America, the goldfields of Western Australia in their infancy were particularly law abiding. This is despite the very few policemen assigned to keep order over large areas. Where there were no policemen in new mining centres or goldrushes, they had their own method of dealing with those who stepped out of line – the 'roll up'.

The procedure of a 'roll-up' was simple and effective. The wronged party would beat a loud tattoo on his panning-off dish, frying pan or kerosene tin and the diggers would gather to help settle the dispute. The offences were generally theft, claim-jumping, or partnership disagreements.

In 1894, a rich alluvial discovery that was ninety-five kilometres east of Kalgoorlie was the scene of one such roll-up. It involved two men, Bull and Winter, who had worked as partners on a lease in Mentor's

'Roll-up': The Law of the Diggers

Gully. Winter argued that Bull was not doing his share of the work and they dissolved their partnership. Winter continued working the lease and Bull took a job with a local tradesman.

Winter found it difficult working the show alone, so he asked a man named Ruse to join the venture on a half-share basis. Ruse was not impressed with the offer and said the show was only a duffer. Winter then confided to him that he had found some good slugs on the lease while Bull was still a partner. One slug was 620-grams. He had not mentioned the finds to his partner, and he gave the gold to the local storekeeper, Tom Bower to send home to his wife.

Ruse went to Bull and told him what Winter had confided. Furious at his former mate's double-dealing, Bull confronted Winter and demanded his share of the gold. Winter eventually admitted the charge but refused to give restitution.

Bull grabbed a tin dish and beat a load and insistent tattoo on it. It was a Sunday morning, and most men were in their camps or out in the street, as no self-respecting digger worked on the Sabbath Day. A large crowd soon gathered. Bull climbed onto a wagon and told the men of his mate's crime. Cries of "string him up" and "hang him" came from among the crowd, who classed cheating a mate as one of the blackest of crimes.

The men decided to hold a trial there and then. They chose a judge, and all those present acted as the jury. A prospector named Billy Mentor offered his services as Bull's barrister, but no one came forward as counsel for Winter. That unhappy man, who became unhappier as the trial progressed, suffered the ignominy of being

'Roll-up': The Law of the Diggers

forced to stand in a buggy with a rope tied around his neck and the other knotted to a beam projecting from a nearby store.

When asked to plead, Winter faltered 'not guilty', but after Bull's counsel had given evidence and the storekeeper confirmed receiving slugs from the accused to send to his wife, it was obvious to those present his plea was a false one. Other evidence was provided, and then Winter attempted an unconvincing defence. The judge summed up the case and asked for a show of hands. When he called out 'guilty', a forest of hands shot into the air.

The judge asked the crowd to suggest an appropriate sentence. An angry, rough minority wanted to hang the guilty man, but the majority opposed such a drastic measure. Several arguments and fights broke out. Seeing all the violence being enacted in front of him, Winter feared for his life.

Two well-known and respected men addressed the crowd and pleaded with them not to go ahead with their violent threats. They argued killing the man would spoil the "fields record as having the most law-abiding miners in the world". They also warned that the Government would react strongly against the introduction of lynch law in Australia.

Common-sense soon prevailed, and the diggers worked out the man's punishment. Winter was marched to his camp and forced to make restitution as far as possible to Bull. They let him pack sufficient food and water and was then roughly marched out of town.

This story appeared in several goldfields' newspapers, so wherever the offender went, someone knew of his crime. He eventually had to leave the State.

'ROLL-UP': THE LAW OF THE DIGGERS

A roll-up of a lighter nature occurred in the Gordon mining camp in the Kanowna district one evening in 1896. The baker, Mr Catchpole, discovered a three-kilogram cake missing from his premises. He went to the tent of the man he suspected of stealing the cake and found him eating the evidence as quickly as he could. The baker called in other miners as witnesses. There had been many other items going missing in the camp, including weapons, so they searched the suspect's camp. They found two stolen guns and a six-chamber revolver hidden within his tent. They then called a 'roll-up'.

The diggers voted a man called Lynch to act as judge. Evidence was given but when the trial was over it was discovered he had left camp, no doubt anticipating a guilty verdict. The thwarted miners administered justice by pulling down the man's tent and then burning his bough-shed and personal belongings. The sweet-toothed thief was not seen in that district again.

In 1898 another roll-up settled a claim dispute at a rush on Block 48, which was close to the present town of Kambalda. Two miners who shared a dryblower and always seemed to help each other, pegged two individual but adjoining leases of twenty-one metres each. One man believed the men should have only pegged a partner's claim of thirty by thirty metres, so he jumped twelve metres of their ground and pegged it out.

A roll-up was called, and the judge chosen for the occasion gave the verdict in favour of the jumper. Most of the diggers thought it was an unwise decision and decided not to ask the same man to take the position of chairman or judge again.

'ROLL-UP': THE LAW OF THE DIGGERS

Dinny O'Callaghan gave an account of 'The Rattling of the Tin Dishes" when he was at the Lake Darlow Rush in 1895. A man was accused of stealing food from another man's camp, which was considered a grave crime. The trial was not going well for him, someone suggesting lynching him from a tree halfway through it. Dinny defended the man, stating that the only evidence they had come from an unreliable Aboriginal tracker that was hanging around the camp. He said they all had similar boots, so it was flimsy evidence to convict a man on. Most of the group agreed and let the man go. The man later thanked Dinny and swore to him that he did not take the food (O'Callaghan 75).

Roll-ups were also used for other purposes. James Balzano records in his diary on Sunday, September 29, 1895:

> At 7.15pm a man named James sounded the tocsin by beating a digger's dish with a little stick, and at the same time he cried "Roll up, roll up". 21 men in all (including myself) turned up. We stood in a circle around a blazing fire, and the man with the dish said: "Well, there is a chap named Proctor very bad with scurvy three weeks, and he wants to go down to the Coolgardie hospital, but he has no money, so I leave it to you what to do." A voice, "He has a mate." "Yes - but his mate is not getting any gold." Then the dish was passed around, some put in silver coins, others piece of gold, myself too contributed my mite, thus nearly £6 was collected today September 30th. The men camping in the New Gully contributed £3.5 - total £9.5.0. Proctor is leaving for Coolgardie tomorrow (Compton & Manners, p41).

By 1903, the custom of calling roll-ups for settling disputes had practically died out. One of the last rollups took place in a little mining town on the railway line between Kalgoorlie and Leonora called

'Roll-up': The Law of the Diggers

Goongarrie. The best of the gold had been mined by this time, and the town was in decline.

It was a Sunday with the dryblowers, and other miners heard the unaccustomed clamour of a beaten tin dish signifying a roll-up. The sound let them to the Mechanic's Institute where they learnt that a well-known agitator, Cadwallader, was charging his mate Atkinson with stealing the contents of the joint 'poverty pot'. This was obtained by dollying prospects taken from a parcel of stone that the partners had recently put through the battery.

The accuser said that there were at least twelve to fifteen grams in the pot and his mate had gone on a trip to Menzies and spent the proceed on 'wine, women and song'. Atkinson indignantly denied the charge and claimed there was never more than two grams in the pot and he had handed it over to Cadwallader in any case. Atkinson was more than willing to be tried there and then in the good old way.

A well-known prospector name Wallace McGorkill took the chair as judge and twelve men were chosen as the jury. The case lasted two hours, mainly because of all the leg-pulling, as no-one took it very seriously. It was an entertaining way to spend an otherwise dull Sunday evening.

The judge finally gave the verdict – both men were fined ten shillings each. Cadwallader for bringing forth a frivolous charge and Atkinson for not having kept his mate posted as to the result of his dollyings.

Chapter Eight

1897 Tragedy Cost Six Lives

UNDERGROUND MINING HAS always been a hazardous occupation, particularly in the early days. The first major underground disaster on the Western Australian goldfields occurred at the Mount Charlotte mine on the Kalgoorlie field in 1897.

It was near the end of an afternoon shift on 8 April 1897. On the ninety-metre level, Charles Milson was preparing to lower blasting charges down twenty-four metres to a man named Rowe. Rowe had already drilled holes in the ore-body for the charges. Four other men, Frank McAdam, William McGauchy, John Murphy and John Wickercraft, were working near Milson. Ken Wilson and William Gibb were working on the sixty-metre level.

While assembling the dynamite charges, Milson used a candle for a light fixed to a 'spider'. A 'spider', or miner's candlestick was a double loop of wire with a hook. The miner usually attached this to the front of his hatband or hung it in a convenient spot near where he was working. Milson had placed his candle inside the wooden box containing the dynamite. He left it there while he went to lower the charges to Rowe. The candle had burnt low and slipped through the spider into the box. When he returned, he saw the dynamite had ignited, so he quickly snatched the candle out of the box and threw it away. Unfortunately, he was too late as the dynamite was already burning.

A box of detonators had begun exploding due to the heat. Wilson and the men working near him rushed to the shaft in a panic. They urgently rang for the cage to lift them to safety, but they did not give the correct signal. Without waiting for it to arrive, they dashed over to the ladderway and began climbing. They shouted out to the other two men on the sixty-metre level, so they too joined the desperate upward climb.

The climb to the surface seemed never-ending. Suffocating fumes in the shaft from the exploding detonators caused two men to collapse on a landing. When the others reached the surface and gasped out their news, volunteers went down into the fumes to help them up.

The underground manager heard the commotion while getting ready for bed. He ran to the shaft, and when he saw the distressed, coughing men, he sent someone to his home to get some painkillers. His wife could not find any, so she gave him a bottle of eucalyptus oil instead. Finally, someone produced a bottle of brandy. After having a drink, the men went to their respective camps.

In the panic, the men forgot about Rowe who was still underground.

Fortunately, he was not affected by the fumes as he was at a lower level. He was brought up later when the underground manager inspected the workings. The fire had burnt itself out, and the fumes had dissipated. As it happened, the forgotten miner was the luckiest of them all.

The next morning, a very sick Milson was taken to the Government hospital where he died two hours later. One of the town's doctors, Dr Gibson became alarmed for the safety of the other men so visited them in their camps. He advised them all to go to the hospital, and four heeded his advice ("Sensational Accident – Death of a Miner", *The Inquirer and Commercial News* [Perth], 9 April 1897].

John Murphy died in St John of God's hospital not long after admittance. Frank McAdam went to the Government hospital and was not expected to last the night. The news quickly spread throughout the town, so McGauchy's friends took him into St John's hospital where he was soon joined by John Wickercraft.

On Thursday evening Ken Wilson died suddenly at his home. Wickercraft died in the early hours of Friday morning, and McGauchy died on Saturday afternoon. The death toll was now at five. Frank McAdam seemed better and was discharged from hospital but relapsed and died ("Fatal Mining Accident", *The Goldfields Morning Chronicle* [Coolgardie], 2 April 1897, p2).

William Gibb refused to go to the hospital. He stayed with some mates who were camped on the higher ground of the Monte Cristo lease. A newspaper reporter visited him there and found him sitting in the open air with his friends. This tall young man, though looking ill and

1897 TRAGEDY COST SIX LIVES

coughing, said he was getting better quickly. He felt that this improvement was caused by the fresh air on the 'heights' where he stayed day and night. One of his mates said, 'It was your tough lungs that pulled you through, Bill'. His recovery slowed down, however, and later he went home to Victoria with forty pounds given to him by the townspeople who had raised money for the families and victims of the disaster.

Reports of the whole affair were given to the District Inspector of Mines, Mr Lightly, and an inquiry was held. Evidence at the hearing showed that if the men had stepped out a metre or so to an open-air shaft close by, remained near the main shaft where the air was fresh, or lain down beneath the level of the fumes, no lives would have been lost. However, it was the fear of explosion that caused the men to do the fatal climb ("Terrible Accident at Kalgoorlie", *Coolgardie Mining Review,* 3 April 1897, p13).

Two lessons were learned from the disaster. Firstly, more inspections of mine sites needed to be made by mining inspectors and secondly, managers and others in charge would have to learn first-aid as taught by the St John's association. An editorial by the *Kalgoorlie Miner* stated that if a trained person had made proper efforts to clear the men's lungs when they reached the surface, some lives might have been saved.

Members of the community raised funds for the widows and children of the deceased. Donations from locals were made at the Kalgoorlie Miner Office, and Mr W J Cotter and Mr J G Alderdice managed to raise £138 5s 6d. As Murphy and Milson were members of the Kalgoorlie Boulder's Workers Association, a levy of one-shilling was made upon the members, and a further fifty pounds was provided from the association for the two families. The Kalgoorlie Men's Social Club and the Committee of the Miners Institute also arranged a performance of "Caste" to raise funds ("The Mount Charlotte Disaster", *Kalgoorlie Miner,* 3 April 1897, p4).

Chapter Nine

Her Final Walk

IT WAS CHRISTMAS MORNING 1915, and a little old lady dressed in a tweed suit was sitting on a seat at the Kalgoorlie railway station. She was waiting for her son, Duncan d'Everylns to come and take her out to his home in Bulong, thirty-two kilometres away. Her name was Mrs Margaret Quinn, and she had just arrived on the express from Perth. Two days prior she arrived in Fremantle from Scotland on the steamship Osterley.

As the hours passed, Mrs Quinn became increasingly anxious and disappointed. By midday, she realised that her son was not coming to get her. She decided that if she was to spend any portion of Christmas day with her son, she had to find her own way to Bulong.

In the meantime, her son was enjoying a quiet Christmas with friends, unaware that he was only thirty-two kilometres from his waiting mother. He did not know that she had left Scotland, let alone arrived in Australia. There had been some correspondence between them several months earlier, but nothing definite had been arranged. He had warned her to be sure to let him know when she intended making the journey. He had also explained that it was only a small mining town that was some distance from Kalgoorlie.

Bulong had been a fair-sized mining town in its heyday at the turn of the century. The main mine, Queen Margaret, had ceased company mining in 1908 and the town was in decline. With many men fighting in the Great War, the town was quieter than ever. Her son was the local school teacher.

The road was the only link between the two towns, as Bulung was not part of the Loopline rail link. On the Kalgoorlie platform, Mrs Quinn made enquiries about travelling to Bulong. She was told that a coach would be going out there on the following Tuesday, three days away. They advised her to take a room and communicate with her son. She apparently booked a room but did not use it. She considered going by taxi, but on learning that the fair was two-pounds ten-shillings, she decided to walk, even though she had six pounds concealed in her jacket. She told the railway authorities that her luggage would be arriving later and asked them to hold it for her. She left the station carrying a small parcel, a parasol and a heavy jacket hanging over one arm.

The dirt roads to Kanowna, Bulong and Mount Monger all branched out from Austral Road, east of Kalgoorlie. At about half-past one a 'little old lady' knocked on the door of Mrs Victoria Quigley's house on Austral Road and asked which road went to Bulong. She told Mrs Quigley about her journey out from Scotland and how there had been no-one at the station to meet her. Mrs Quigley asked: "But you're not going to walk to Bulong?" to which she replied, "Yes I am". Mrs Quigley asked her if she knew how far it was, to which she replied, "sixteen miles", even though she had been told it was twenty miles. The local woman tried to dissuade her from attempting the long walk as it was over one-hundred degrees, but Mrs Quinn insisted that the taxi fare was too expensive and she must get there today.

Harold Jackson, a clerk employed by the Chamber of Mines, was feeling unwell so was resting on a bed on the neighbouring front verandah. He overheard the conversation between the two women. Mrs Jackson watched her from her gate, surprised to see an elderly lady in heavy clothing walk past all the houses in town. Due to the heat and her inappropriate clothing, Harold became concerned about the lone walker. Despite his illness, he got on his motorbike and found her two kilometres down the road. The young man tried to persuade her to return to town as it was a sweltering day and there were no houses or water near the track. She advised him that the taxi fare was too expensive, and she couldn't wait three days for the coach. She was determined to continue as she wanted to see her son for Christmas. He could not convince her of the danger, so he warned her to stay on the road. He consoled himself with the thought that some vehicle would soon come along and give her a lift, as there was generally traffic on the road. However, no vehicles came as it was Christmas afternoon.

Three days later, on Tuesday morning, Mounted Constable Duggan was on patrol on Austral Parade when he was stopped by Mrs King, who also lived on Austral Parade. She told him about Mrs Quinn and her concerns about her. She asked the constable if he could check whether the old lady had made it to her son's house safely. The policeman telephoned Duncan d'Everlyns and was informed that he had not seen his mother. Ironically, he had only just received a letter from a friend in Scotland a few minutes earlier advising him that his mother had left Scotland on 17 November (*Kalgoorlie Western Argus*, 4 Jan 1916, p21).

Mr d'Everlyns and several of his friends began a search from the Bulong end of the road while Constable Duggan and two Aboriginal trackers started searching for the old lady's tracks leading out from Kalgoorlie. They discovered the tracks about six kilometres from town, but they disappeared. The trackers thought she may have been given a lift. As there was no evidence of this, they continued the search the next day. The tracks were picked up again two kilometres farther on and showed that she had left the road and begun heading north. That day and the next were spent searching for and following tracks. By New Year's Eve, the men were following signs of an erratic course made by a terrified, confused and exhausted woman.

On New Year's Day the police, trackers, her son and others in the volunteer search party assembled at the point they had finished at the previous night. The area was flat, rough, iron-stone country. At night the lights from the mines on the Golden Mile would have been clearly visible to anyone standing there. The men carefully kept behind the trackers so their footprints would not interfere with the problematic trail they were following through dried grass with stony patches. When they were about sixteen kilometres from Kalgoorlie and nearly six kilometres north-east of the Bulong road, a tracker named Jacky said "she's getting tired", and ten metres away they found her body.

Her Final Walk

It was a week after she set off on her walk to Bulong when her body was found lying underneath a shrub beside an old bush track. She had discarded her hat, and her white hair hung loosely about her blackened face. She had removed her tweed jacket and skirt to lay on and was lying on her side like she was sleeping. Her open umbrella had a broken handle as if she had fallen on it at some point. Her son dropped to his knees, kissed her and said, "It is my mother".

In her bag was a letter from her son giving explicit instructions on how to proceed. It stated she should tell him when she was arriving so he could make the necessary arrangements. They also found the six pounds concealed in her jacket.

A newspaper reporter described the finding of her body a "pathetic climax to one of the most pathetic cases of this nature that has engaged the attention of the Kalgoorlie police."

At the inquest, the Coroner brought in a verdict of accidental death and said, "She evidently did not know the nature of the death-trap she was walking into." In those few words, he summed up this sad story of a woman who came from a small, well-populated country who had no concept of the isolation, vastness and danger of the Australian bush (*Kalgoorlie Western Argus*, 11 Jan 1916 p21); (*Sunday Times* [Perth] 9 Jan 1916).

Her Final Walk

Chapter Ten

The Happy Loopline Train

LOCAL RESIDENT JACK DOYLE claimed that if there had been a competition to find the happiest train in the world, "the old Loopline would have won hands down".

This unique railway was laid down around the eastern goldfields' Golden Mile, and in the twenty-odd years of its operation, it was one of the busiest railways in Australia. It enabled the efficient movement of people and goods between Boulder, Kalgoorlie and their outlying suburbs.

The first portion of the line was built in 1897, only a year after the railway from Perth to Kalgoorlie was completed. At first, it was planned as an 'ore tramway' to convey the large and increasing quantities of firewood, timber, stores, machinery, and other necessary equipment to the developing mines of the Golden Mile.

The Happy Loopline Train

The Premier, the Minister for Mines and the Commissioner for Public Works, Mr F H Piesse, went to Kalgoorlie to discuss the project with local public bodies. These bodies were the Municipal Council, the Chamber of Mines, the Institute of Mine Managers, the Roads Board, and the Kalgoorlie and Boulder Workers' Association. From their discussions, they agreed upon a line starting from Kalgoorlie that would then go close to the mines to a railway station at Boulder. From there it would go to Hannan's Lake and the old Leviathan battery. A spur line was to extend to the Boulder townsite, which was then in the process of construction. Mr Piesse later decided that this was "objectionable from a railway point of view" and that the line should go directly to the Boulder townsite.

Mr F Wittenoom, the chairman of the Progress Committee, had earlier told residents at a public meeting that they should resist any scheme to connect Boulder with Kalgoorlie for at least twelve months, "for the sake of trade at the Boulder". The other members of the committee apparently did not agree, because at a meeting held a month later they commended the Government's decision to link their town with the railway.

The committee considered the flat country near the town suitable for shunting purposes and urged the Government "to use all speed in completing the line via town to Boulder and thence to Hannan's Lake". The Government's change of plan and its decision to build the line directly to Boulder upset a lot of people, so they held a meeting in Kalgoorlie's Tivoli Gardens. They were concerned that the new route would avoid the Lake View, Ivanhoe, and Boulder mines as well as the Haycraft battery and Zeb Lane's public crusher.

The Happy Loopline Train

A compromise was finally reached, and on 8 November 1897 two lines were opened. One was for the use of passenger and goods trains that ran to Boulder from Kalgoorlie via Kallaroo and Golden Gate. The track then curved around east to Kamballie and finished at Lakeside. The second line was used for carrying timber and goods to the mines and branched out from Golden Gate, not far from the previous site of the Hainault tourist mine (that is now part of the Super Pit). It went through the mines to Kamballie with several shunting lines leading into the sidings of the various mines.

A few months after the first section of the Loopline had been completed, one of the trains was used to transport a severely injured man from the Kallaroo siding into the Kalgoorlie District Hospital. He was Henry Joseph Dower, the twenty-three-year-old identical twin of my great-great-grandfather. The young man had been injured while shaft-sinking in the Eclipse mine and died a day or two later.

Work on the lines was not finished by the time of the official opening. At a municipal meeting in Kalgoorlie on 1 November, members reported that the contractors were using auriferous (gold-bearing) cement from the Monte Cristo lease as ballast. They passed a resolution to inform the Minister of this fact, and that ballast should be obtained elsewhere.

The locals took immediate advantage of the new train service. During the last week of November 1897, nine-thousand passengers used the line. While they were delighted with their new mode of transport, many complained about the tardiness of the Government not providing shelter on the Hannan Street platform. A significant number of passengers used this station as it was more convenient than the central station at the end of Wilson Street. Two local businessmen solved the problem by having a temporary six by five-metre shelter built. These community-minded gentlemen were W J Reynolds of the Grand Hotel and a draper named J H Pellew.

There were hopes that the Loopline circling the mines would be completed within a few weeks, but the Railways Department had other commitments, and it was 1902 before it was finalised. The delay particularly annoyed mine owners and citizens on the eastern outskirts of the town. Several made submissions to the Government on the subject.

There was more fuss in 1900 when Hannan Street businessmen heard that the new brick station buildings planned for the Hannan Street station were to be erected on a new site, between Egan and McDonald Streets. A deputation travelled to Perth to argue the matter, and a compromise was reached. The railway station with its imposing main entrance was built in Hannan Street, and the smaller opening in the fence at the top of Egan Street was left.

In March 1901, work started on the second section of the Loopline. The workmen began their tasks at both ends of the section. Around one-hundred men using twenty drays were engaged on the earthworks alone. There were difficulties in obtaining some materials as well as sufficient rolling stock. There were complaints about the general shortage of railway trucks on the goldfields.

However, the engineer, Mr Tindale and the works manager, Jas F McGregor, pushed the work ahead as fast as conditions allowed. It was expected that the job would be completed within six months, but it wasn't until 17 March the following year the line was officially opened.

A second set of rails from Coolgardie to Kalgoorlie and then to Kamballie was also put down around this time. Island platforms with brick station buildings and station-masters' houses were constructed at Hannan Street, Kallaroo, Golden Gate, Kamballie and Boulder. The contractors also built a large brick station building on the two-sided main platform and an island platform connected by an overhead bridge at Boulder. At Hannan Street, Golden Gate, and Kamballie, there were brick-lined subways through which patrons could safely walk to the station platforms on the other side. There were signal boxes on all stations up to Kamballie, but none from there on.

An extra line went south-east from Kamballie to Lakeside, and the Loopline then curved around and headed north past the old Ivanhoe (later the Imperial) mine, and then onto Trafalgar, Hill End, Brown Hill, Croesus, and Williamstown. It met and joined the line again just past the Williamstown crossing, completing the loop. The stations on the Eastern side were all single sided and less pretentious than those on the western section.

The round trip from the Kalgoorlie Station was about thirteen kilometres and took around forty-five minutes. During 1902-1903, the thousands of patrons enjoyed more services than those living in the metropolitan area. On weekdays, some thirty trains provided a return service from Kalgoorlie to Kamballie, via Boulder, with thirty-three on Saturdays and twenty-seven on Sundays. About half this number continued around the outer circle through Brown Hill. Three or four trains ran out to Lakeside from Kamballie daily. With such a high volume of traffic, it is easy to see why every station needed its own stationmaster and staff.

Some of the early carriages had a corridor down one side which opened into 'dog-dox' compartments, but most of them were Gilbert carriages with a central aisle between rows of wooden seats. The carriages were pulled by 'Nellies', N Class 4-4-4T steam engines.

One of the early conductors who collected tickets on the Loopline was George Bennetts. He later became well known as a senior conductor on the Trans-train, councillor in local government and Member of the Legislative Council. He remembered the crowded carriages being lit at night by oil lamps which used peanut oil as fuel.

Another resident has vivid memories of the clatter of feet on the carriage roofs at night. This clatter was made by a porter whose job was to drop the lighted lamps down into position from the top of each carriage. She also remembers travelling with her brother in an end carriage that was left in darkness. When they stepped out at Boulder they received curious looks from some other travellers. Her brother then explained to her that they had been sitting in the "Lovers' Carriage".

The suburbs of Kamballie, Trafalgar, Hill End, Brown Hill, and Williamstown sprang up on and near mining leases, as the mine workers preferred living near their places of work. Between 1908 and 1909, their population was around four-thousand. Kamballie was already in decline, with only twenty houses left. Brown Hill had one-hundred-and-fifty-three homes, a hotel, fire-station, several shops, hall, brick school, convent school, churches, post office and football

The Happy Loopline Train

oval. Trafalgar was larger and had more than twice the number of houses, similar facilities, a street of shops and two hotels. The Trafalgar oval had a large grandstand with a wooden picket fence and was the home ground for the Mines Football Club.

Around this time a football team had arrived from Perth to play a combined team of the district. It was arranged for one of the teams to wear the Mines Club guernseys. Jack Doyle's father was the Mines Football Club's property man. He was having a drink in a local hotel while waiting for the train to take him to the big match in Kalgoorlie. He had the football guernseys with him packed in a large bag. He tarried a little too long in the hotel and was startled to hear the train whistle as it left the Trafalgar station.

In a panic, he ran over to the railway line and in the middle of the train track took out one of the football guernseys. He waved it frantically at the approaching train. The engine was pulling about a dozen carriages, all packed with football supporters. The train was on a downgrade when the driver slammed on the brakes. Luckily the train stopped in time, and Doyle clambered aboard to the amusement of the football supporters. Fortunately for Mr Doyle, the football team received their guernseys in time for the match.

This was also the era of brass bands and several bandsmen who travelled on the Loopline often entertained passengers by playing their instruments on the train. Tassie Jacobs was a regular passenger and played his cornet for the passengers. This usually resulted in a sing-song and those living near the bends of the track could hear the music above the noise of the old steam train.

The Happy Loopline Train

At this time, the shops remained open until 9pm on Saturdays. The 'suburbanites' generally made Saturday their main night out and caught the Loopline train into Kalgoorlie or Boulder. The men often visited one of the pubs while the rest of the family went shopping, met friends, went to a live show or to the pictures. Saturday-night movies attracted large crowds, but sometimes the last train home for the eastern suburbs would leave before the end of the movie. If the train looked like beating the film, Tom Doyle and his sister would stand at the front door of the theatre, half-watching the movie while listening anxiously for the sound of the train as it left the central station.

As the years went by, the population of the eastern suburbs declined. By 1922, the only passenger train running on the east portion of the line was a rail motor coach nicknamed the 'Tin Hare'. This limited service continued for about another ten years. The Kalgoorlie to Boulder line remained open, mainly for goods traffic. In the 1960's this line also closed, marking the end of the old Loopline.

Except for Williamstown near Kalgoorlie, all these suburbs have since disappeared. There is nothing left at Kamballie. As of 1980, the old station platform and one lonely house were all that was left standing at Trafalgar, or 'Traf' as its former residents affectionately called it.

In 1978 two railway enthusiasts, Bryan Smith and Mike Wheeler, determined there was enough interest for a weekend tourist run to be viable. The Loopline Society restored a dining car purchased from Westrail, and in 1982 the Loopline commenced full-time operations. It used the dining car and ex-WA Government Railways coaching stock and locomotives. However, in January 2004, KCGM claimed the track for the expansion of the current Super Pit operations, thus ending the working history of the 'happiest train' in Australia.

There is hope that the spirit of the 'happiest train' will be resurrected soon, so one day you may be able to travel on it. On its website in 2018, the Golden Mile Loopline Railway Society states:

> We are planning out future designs to incorporate and build new tracks, stages are listed for improvement:
>
> Stage 1: Boulder to the Superpit Lookout;
>
> Stage 2: Top end of Hannan St - WA Museum;
>
> Stage 3: Hannan's North Tourist Mine" (Golden Mile Loopline Railway Society) (Golden Mile Loopline Railway Society)

Chapter Eleven

The Fabulous Londonderry

EVERY PROSPECTOR'S DREAM IS TO FIND a reef held together with gold. Among the few whose dreams were realised was a group of men from Queensland, being John Mills, Thomas Elliott, John Huxley, William Gardiner, Henry Dawson, and Peter Carter. These men pooled their resources together and travelled to Coolgardie to try their luck on the new goldfield.

Bayley and Ford discovered gold there in September 1892. News quickly spread around Australia and there was a gold rush to the area. By the time the above gentlemen arrived from Queensland, most of the alluvial gold had been cleaned out. Prospectors then fanned out in all directions searching for the precious metal. A successful find would mean the difference between living the life of a gentleman or returning to the drudgery of their former existence.

With their horse and cart piled high with equipment, they journeyed through the bush in search of the precious metal. Elliott and Huxley had prospecting experience from Victoria, but the remainder had no prospecting or mining experience.

When returning from this unsuccessful prospecting trip, they decided to part company. Their feelings towards each other at this moment were far from friendly. Perhaps the thought of returning home with no fortune caused frayed tempers.

It was May 1894 when they were south-east of Coolgardie near Lake Lefroy. They decided to split up and meet again in Coolgardie to sell their equipment and share the proceeds before returning to Eastern Australia.

Mill and his mate left together on the 13 May and decided to cross some low hills. They were then about twenty kilometres from Coolgardie picking their way over a quartz outcrop. The two men stopped to talk, and Mills began idly tapping at a piece of rock with his knapping hammer. When the rock broke away, they saw it was held together with gold!

They quickly fired a couple of sticks of dynamite into the quartz and as soon as the flying stones settled they rushed back to see gold gleaming throughout the broken rock. They knew this would make them all rich. Forgetting their differences, the pair dashed off to find the other four men to tell them the excellent news.

When the excitement had died down, and the men had pegged their claim, they decided to work the find secretly for as long as possible. They knew that as soon as they applied for the lease at the warden's

The Fabulous Londonderry

office in Coolgardie, news of the find would quickly spread causing a rush to the field. Before this happened, they wanted to get as much gold out as they could.

They broke off a lot of gold from the outcrop, but the cautious amongst them called a halt while the pot-hole was still showing ribs and knuckles of gold. They went a little distance off the outcrop and started a shaft to cut out the reef at a depth of fifty feet. At forty-two feet they put in a short crosscut and hit the golden stone as rich as it was on the surface.

The reef was only one to two metres wide, and all the gold seemed to be in one pocket. The stone, thickly seamed with gold up to six millimetres thick, was taken out of one hole. This became known as the Golden Hole. The men named their find the Londonderry, probably as most of them were Irish.

4,000 to 5,000 ounces was won in a few days. 'Big Ben,' one famous piece of quartz that was later taken out from the surface weighed 240 pounds. It was valued at £3,500.

They packed the precious stones in five swags and threw it on an old cart they had. Two of the party took the precious load into the bank. Records show that on 23 June 1894, the party lodged 4,280 ounces of gold in Coolgardie (Costeen, "Famous Londonderry Strike Recalled" *Kalgoorlie Miner,* 9 December 1946, p1). They purchased supplies and returned. Their find was still undiscovered as the officials did not know the precise location, although secret whispers escaped the bank gold-room.

After a few weeks, the men became nervous that someone would discover their golden treasure and jump their claim. Once a claim is pegged, within ten days the necessary papers must be lodged at the warden's office. If this doesn't occur, anyone can 'jump' the claim and re-peg it. They agreed that two of them should go to Coolgardie and hire an agent to do the necessary business for them. The man they chose was told it was 'just bit of a show' and asked him not to talk about this find to anyone.

On 11 May 1894, they applied for a lease of twenty-five acres. Evidently, they made some mistake, as the prospectors were only granted a lease of fifteen-acres, three-roods and twenty-two-poles. The prospectors formed themselves into a syndicate with sixty shares, which they shortly afterwards increased to 960.

It turned out that one of their own men gave the game away. He became ill and went into Coolgardie for treatment with a few of the spectacular specimens in his pockets. Unfortunately, he first went to a hotel where he prescribed for himself a few too many whiskies. He boasted he was the wealthiest man on the 'fields and showed off his specimens. The news of the fabulous find was out within hours.

Anyone who could walk or ride arrived at the Londonderry and pegged every centimetre of ground for kilometres around the original claim. This was where Dennis O'Callaghan pegged the ground where Mill's party had pitched its tents and hut. The hut held the bags of rich specimen stone that had to be guarded day and night ("The Story of the Londonderry", *The Sun* [Kalgoorlie], 10 November 1907, p9).

Although it is impossible to know the exact amount, it was estimated that 106,000 grams of gold were extracted from the hole within six weeks and lodged in the bank at Coolgardie. This would have been worth around £40,000. The newspapers spread the news to the outside world, using phrases such as 'A mountain of gold', 'One of the Wonders of the World', and 'The Greatest Discovery that Australia Has Known'. One reporter thought that the sale of all this gold should be restricted to avoid flooding the market, which would cause the world price of gold to fall.

Despite all the dryblowing by so many diggers in the area, few shared in the wealth. Those who were unsuccessful felt a great deal of resentment towards the original finders for keeping the news to themselves for so long and not giving others a chance.

Discord broke out again amongst the owners of the Londonderry. Three members of the party sold their shares to the remainder for £3,000 each.

Offers began to pour in from promoters and companies wanting to buy the claim. An offer of £25,000 was refused. However, becoming tired of guarding their bonanza, the three owners sold it to a syndicate represented by Lord Fingall for £180,000 cash and a one-sixth interest in paid-up shares. The cash consideration was thirty times greater than that paid to Bayley and Ford for their mine in Coolgardie.

The men then returned to Eastern Australia. Mills bought a farm and married a girl who had helped fund the prospecting trip.

In September 1894, a ceremony was held at the mine to celebrate the purchase, with around fifty men and several V.I.P.'s in attendance. The Mayor of Coolgardie, Mr J Shaw, who was also the acting manager for the owners of the mine, uncovered the reef. A parcel of stone was then broken out and packed in boxes to send to England. The stone studded with gold included some of the richest taken out of the property.

The boxes were valued at about £12,000 and held 530 kilograms of quartz. They were sealed in the presence of the warden in readiness to be taken back to England by Lord Fingall. He was returning to form a company and raise money to develop the mine. A few days later, Lord Fingall left De Baun's hotel in a special Cobb & Co coach, accompanied by an escort. After staying in Perth for a few days as a guest of the Governor-General, he sailed for England.

The stone from the Londonderry was put on exhibition in London, where it created great excitement, as they were some of the best specimens the world had seen. A company was soon formed, and £700,000 of capital was raised to develop the mine. Coolgardie's first mayor, James Shaw, cleared £10,000 on his share transaction. He had purchased 40 shares off Thomas Elliott for £1000 on 4 August 1894 ("The Famous Londonderry", *Kalgoorlie Western Argus,* 5 May 1914, p8).

The cutting was then covered with a steel plate and cemented down, and the two-metre fence that had been built around it was securely locked. The key was handed over to Warden Finnerty, and a man was appointed to protect the property night and day. General development of the reef occurred, but work on the Golden Hole was deferred until Lord Fingall's return from England.

A town and business centre soon sprang up. W H Lindsay built the first hotel, which he called Londonderry. Mr Lindsay was one of the early settlers on the Coolgardie fields and at one time acted as agent for the original prospectors.

As the development of the mine proceeded, patches of rich ore were met with at varying depths down to around two-hundred feet. Some pockets were extremely rich. A parcel of ore was sold to the Government for exhibition in Paris. The total weight of it was between twelve and thirteen hundred ounces, and the gold content would have smelted over four hundred ounces.

Over more than a year, the mine provided plenty of excitement as rich patches were disclosed from time to time. However, its life was short and its end inglorious because apart from a small area of enrichment, the reef was poor.

Lord Fingall returned from England on 28 March 1895. On that day he and the Managing Director, R S Black, opened the Golden Hole. Those also present were the mine manager, Mr G Aarons, the foreman, Bill Watty, Tom Duff, and Carpenter.

After clearing the hole of the debris with which it had been filled, a careful inspection was made to satisfy themselves that no sample holes had been put down by the prospectors. As the quartz in the bottom was unbroken and showed coarse gold, the assumption was that the prospectors were entirely unaware that they had practically exhausted the rich surface deposit. Had they gone eight inches deeper they would have seen the gold cut out on a floor of solid, barren quartz. Black's diary entry of that day read, "Result of work most unsatisfactory, the rich stone being apparently almost at an end", and on the following day, "Results no more satisfactory than yesterday". Thus, ended the glory of the Golden Hole.

The Fabulous Londonderry

Two days later, Black and Fingall sent a cable to London bluntly detailing their findings. It arrived on the 1 April but was not disclosed to the public for a few days, as some of the directors were out of town. At the extraordinary general meeting, Fingall was attacked for sending the cable, but it was decided to announce it to the press. The news created a sensation. Fingall received much criticism at home and in London for what was termed precipitate judgment. Shares dropped from thirty-five shillings to fifteen shillings. Despite the announcement, many remained sceptical of his dire outlook for the mine.

The following was reported in *The Inquirer and Commercial News* ([Perth], 12 April 1895, p10):

> The news which was flashed from London that the much sought after and extremely rich Londonderry mine had proved a failure, came like a sudden clap of thunder upon the community, and no less surprise did it create at Coolgardie when the cable message was re-transmitted from Perth. It is hardly credible that nothing was known in the immediate vicinity of the mine as to the alleged sudden collapse of this most wonderful of mines, and even now ... most people are sceptical as to their accuracy. ... The facts, so far as we are able to-gleam them, certainly point to the fact that there must be something wrong somewhere. It will be remembered that after Lord Fingall secured the mine and took from it some of the richest specimens the world has seen, he barricaded the hole from which they were taken and had every means of entrance securely locked and barred. ... Lord Fingall, since his return, could have only done one day's work on the mine, on Friday, March 29 – and upon this the industry of all others which the colony is now dependent to a large extent, is to be dammed, and Coolgardie, as a goldfield, looked upon as

something unclean as not to be touched. It is just possible, but it seems hardly credible with the magnificent show of glittering gold in sight when Lord Fingall left for London, that one more day's work should see the bottom of it. ... Further, why was the mine locked up pending the floatation of the Company! Was it because it was thought that there was a chance of what is now said to have happened being realised before the company could be got off. ...

A London reporter of the time wrote the following:

Nothing quite like this has, we should imagine, ever been known in the history of mining. The average mine manager or mining expert has a natural bent which causes him to soften the shock of disappointment and who is invariably hopeful to the last gasp. Lord Fingall, however, is not built that way, and his cable was a veritable bolt out of the blue. This being so, it is the more to be regretted that the news was not at once made public. Of course, we can quite understand the secretary's reluctance to authorise the publication of the telegram until he had conferred with the board. But meanwhile, in some mysterious way, the news leaked out, and heavy selling of the shares took place (The Londonderry and British Investors", *Western Mail* [Perth], 18 May 1895, p27).

According to the Managing Director of the mine, Lord Fingall never made one shilling out of the Londonderry flotation. He resolutely declined to sell any of his shares, even though strongly urged to do so when the worst had been made known about the mine and shares still held around fifteen shillings. Others may not have been so scrupulous (Black, R. S., "The Londonderry Mine – Its Romantic History" *Western Mail* [Perth], 17 May 1934, p12).

In April 1895, the *Goldfields Courier* headlined 'The Londonderry Collapse'. Further critical newspaper articles caused great consternation among shareholders, and the share price dropped rapidly.

The Times asserted that the rich 'blow' had run out suddenly and that, although blame could not be attached to the promoters, it had been audacious to ask £180,000 for a mine of unknown value. The *Pall Mall Gazette* was more censorious, describing the development of the mine as a sensation boom and the collapse proving how unreliable the experts had been.

Colonel North, who was instrumental in financing the mine, said he would do his best to see that the shareholders got their money back with five per cent interest. He also declared that in his opinion, gold had been stolen from the rich shoot. The mine managed to produce £50,000 worth of gold for the company, which was later taken over by other interests. This was little reward for all the work involved.

The Londonderry, which was a boon to a few and a disappointment to investors, had the lasting effect of attracting a great influx of people to Western Australia. Other new finds, such as the Wealth of Nations, were discovered around Coolgardie soon after. This encouraged many of the gold-seekers to stay in the region. However, none of these finds was another golden hole, so while the memory of other mines has grown dim, people still talk of the fabulous Londonderry.

Chapter Twelve

Wealth of Nations and Dunnsville

MOST OF THE DISAPPOINTED alluvialists from the Londonderry rush returned to Coolgardie in the hope that something would turn up. This hope was realised in August 1894 when an experienced prospector named John Dunn returned from a prospecting trip with camels and an Afghan offsider. Experienced observers noted that the camels' saddlebags were bulging, so they followed Dunn to his destination – the West Australian Bank. Inside, the prospector tipped out gold-encrusted specimen stones. The bank manager then displayed these wonderful stones in the window. These spectacular specimens came from what was to be aptly named the 'Wealth of Nations'.

Dunn's experience and considerable knowledge of geology led him to one of the most notable gold discoveries of Australia. He came from a family of prospectors, and his childhood was spent in the goldfields of Victoria. By the age of fifteen, he was successfully prospecting around Castlemaine. Later he was placed in charge of Government prospecting parties, a position he held for five years. He then undertook private prospecting.

Dunn arrived in Western Australia in 1890, after the promising gold finds in Southern Cross. He was placed in charge of an expedition to explore the interior of Western Australia by a syndicate of private investors. These were Alexander Forrest (Lord Mayor of Perth), W E Marmion, Monger and Co., A W Hassell, Neil McNeil and Crossland.

For about four months he prospected over a vast area of the country with varying luck. Although he was finding some gold, none seemed promising enough to peg out leases. He explored the Murchison and Gascoyne districts before heading south towards Coolgardie.

Occasionally he was troubled by Aboriginals. While at Lake Carey near Mount Weld, numbers of them approached him with warlike demonstrations. To frighten them away, they fired their rifles. No casualties were mentioned.

He discovered an excellent reef located twenty-eight miles north from Coolgardie. He pegged out a lease and named this reef the Brilliant. He worked this mine with his brother until it was floated into a company. They obtained a profitable share in the proceeds of its sale. His brother was satisfied with his profit and decided to retire from prospecting.

Dunn continued exploring for the syndicate, going as far as the South Australian border. Now his only companions were two afghans and camels. They would often not see other people for months on end. In

January 1893 he discovered the True Blue, Sunbeam, and Lone Hand mines. They were close to each other and were purchased by the Lone Hand Mining Company from the prospecting syndicate for £75,000. Dunn received a third of the sale proceeds. He managed and developed these mines until June 1893. At this time the company employed a new manager so that he could continue prospecting.

Dunn obtained enough supplies to last ten months and set off exploring again with his camels and an Afghan assistant. They made their way back to Coolgardie, as he wanted to explore promising country he had seen on previous tours. After days of prospecting, he discovered four-hundred ounces of alluvial gold in a gully near his camp. Nearby there were several outcropping reefs. On 10 August, he broke the cap off a reef that was five feet high and nine feet thick wide. He was astonished to see 'a mountain of gold'. From here he obtained 'the Honest John' specimen, which contained eight-hundred ounces of gold worth £3,000. This was a brilliant specimen of gold in quartz. The whole lode glistened with gold in the sunlight. Within a short period of time, he had £22,000 worth of gold. He aptly named it 'Wealth of Nations".

He now had the problem of getting so much gold safely to the bank and securing his lease. He stowed a little more than half in various places within his travel equipment, even cutting water-bags and casting away precious water. He travelled quietly at night and entered Coolgardie while the electrified mining camp was in slumbers. His Afghan assistant guarded the precious gold while he quickly took out a lease and then deposited the gold in the bank. They promptly returned to the Wealth of Nations with his explorer friend, David

Wealth of Nations and Dunnsville

Lindsay.

He later returned to Coolgardie with the remaining gold. As described previously, the bank manager displayed the gold in the bank's window (Kimberley).

This caused great excitement, men pushed and shoved to see the glittering stones. They asked Dunn where he found them. As his claim was safely lodged at the warden's office, he advised them that they came from the Jaurdi Hills area, some sixty-five kilometres north-west of Coolgardie and that there were thousands of tonnes of the same stuff out there.

The men got hold of every available horse, buggy, cart, bike and barrow and followed Dunn back to his find. The first to reach Dunn's lease was 'Camel' McKenzie, Jack Tierney, Climie, Eastwood, and Martin, who all pegged leases around the original find. Within three days seven-hundred men were already pegging out leases. When the slower-moving prospectors arrived, they found most of the likely claims already pegged.

McKenzie and Tierney had secured the north-end block. Shortly afterwards they were seen cycling madly back into town to send a cable to English investors. They offered their new mine (a shallow costean) for sale at £50,000, and within a week they had received a ten per cent deposit. Lords Sudely and Fingall were cautious and declined the offer, but other Englishmen invested in the unproven ground.

Eastwood and Climie pegged the south end and managed to induce the British to invest in their leases.

Wealth of Nations and Dunnsville

A roll-up was called on the first day of the rush to settle ownership of a slug found by Tom Love. He had picked up the 2,180 gram specimen on John Dunn's line, but this was about one-hundred metres from Dunn's reef. The men decided in favour of Love, who said: "That was the baby, now I'll find the old man". He indeed managed to do this later the same day. He unearthed from farther down the gully a specimen weighing 6,100 grams. He found no more, and rumours spread that Dunn may have planted the slug to keep for himself, as the find belonged to the syndicate.

Shortly after the find, some of the syndicate members, including Forrest, visited the Wealth of Nations. Dunn set off some dynamite for the benefit of his visitors which revealed 'a splendid mass of glittering specimens'. Dunn broke off one of the most significant pieces that were heavy with gold, weighing around 1,870 grams. He handed it to Forrest who then passed it around among the watching crowd. When the stone was given back to Forrest, its appearance had significantly altered. He now had an ordinary rock containing only a few particles of gold. In the row that followed, everyone pleaded innocence. One writer later said that if the actions of three men had been observed the next morning, the mystery would have been solved.

A busy, thriving camp sprang up near the Wealth of Nations that became known as Dunnsville. Two-up was a favourite form of recreation. On one Sunday morning, Lord Fingall put a pound note in the ring, when the Afghan looking after his camels excitedly called him away. Shortly afterwards the punters saw Fingall, his friends and their camels pass by with picks, shovels and other prospecting equipment. 'A rush on', someone shouted. They all grabbed any tools they could find and followed the camels' tracks.

A few kilometres out, the crowd found Lord Fingall thoughtfully examining a quartz outcrop, listening to the Afghan's story of how he had discovered it. The Afghan had been out chasing the camels when he cut through the bushes and saw a white man carefully inspecting the quartz. When the man saw he was being observed, he threw his coat over the spot. The Afghan asked the man to show him what was underneath, so he carefully lifted the jacket to reveal a portion of the reef glistening in the sun. The Afghan then raced back to camp to tell his employer. Lord Fingall and the crowd were disgusted and disappointed when they realised the glittering mass was only mundic. Although they questioned the Afghan, he was unable to describe or identify the hoaxer.

Two-up was not the only form of recreation in the early days of the camp settlement. Practically the whole camp would gather around a massive fire in the evenings and 'spend the hours in song, jest and story'. All those who possessed vocal gifts were expected to contribute, while those whom 'nature had denied such pleasing social qualities' carried wood and looked after the fire. There was even a bush orchestra, which consisted of a camel can drum, steel drilling hoisting plug triangle, comb and paper, two tin whistles and an accordion.

A lot of talent was discovered during these shows. One evening an elderly stranger stepped into the glow of the firelight to contribute his piece. The audience looked at the man's bald head, his flowing beard and solemn face with downcast eyes. They expected him to intone 'The Holy City' or to recite some Shakespeare, but instead, he burst forth into a song of 'the most ribald description'. The 'wicked looking eyes leered in a most suggestive manner' as he sang chorus after chorus of his song and lewd parody. An anonymous writer for the *Sunday Sun* stated:

> He should have sued his appearance for libel. He would have won the case easily, with costs, and even now when I hear the term, 'bald-headed old reprobate', my thoughts fly back to the patriarch of Dunnsville sitting by the blazing logs warbling his infamous contribution.

'Billy the Fowl' was the next performer who delighted the audience with a comic recitation and some bird imitations. "He introduced almost half of the bird life of Australia into the barren and desolate gully, which was taxed to its utmost to support a few lizards." Billy had another side to his character, as he was well versed in scientific matters and spoke three languages fluently. "The latter accomplishment he was wont to use when speaking of and to, the myriads of flies which in those days worked three shifts and never took a Sunday off".

One Sunday, the crowd decided to hold a sports meeting. The hat was passed around for prize money. A handicapper and a judge were appointed, and a program was drawn up. The day was scorching, so the participants disrobed and, obeying that ancient edict, 'lay aside every impediment and ran the race set before them.'

The time came for the finals in the high-jump event, which was between Charlie Island, a well-known back-blocks athlete and Yank, a noted high-jumper and tall-yarn spinner. Just before it started, Yank was suddenly struck with an attack of modesty, ran to his camp and emerged partially clothed. The crowd cheered when they saw that he was clad in a waistcoat, with his legs through the armholes and his rear view covered by the buttoned portion. Island failed in his high-jump attempt but Yank, with a wild Indian war-whoop and a desperate effort, topped the bar – waistcoat and all. He won and got a special award for the best fancy dress.

A few mines opened at Dunnsville and at one time one-thousand men were employed. The Wealth of Nations syndicate took gold to the value of £23,000 before selling it to Colonel North for £146,000.

Workers on a nearby mine were paid their wages each fortnight by the company's attorney, Mr Wymond. He travelled to Dunnsville by horse and buggy from Coolgardie. While there, he also collected the takings that a Scotsman named Aleck made from selling water at the mine. As Aleck could not read or write, he devised a very novel method of keeping his books. He set up stones outside his tent – large stones for gallons and smaller stone for half-gallons. Unfortunately, he had made an enemy of a teamster who would kick and scatter them about when given half a chance. As this would usually happen just before Wymond was due to arrive and collect the money, it caused great confusion and some colourful language.

Dunnsville did not have a long life. One man who had taken part in the early rush visited the town nine years later in September 1903. He climbed to the top of the Wealth of Nations hill and looked around. He said that all that remained on the flat where the township had once stood were scraps of hessian. Dusatoy, the shanty-keeper and the storekeepers Kittley and Tretheway had left. The only mine operating on a small scale was the Wealth of Nations. A man called Jones had purchased it a year before. Like many other little gold mining towns on the Eastern Goldfields, Dunnsville had died.

Chapter Thirteen

Tom Dimer: Son of a Pioneer

TOM DIMER'S LIFE STORY highlights many critical historical developments of Western Australia. He was the son of a pioneer and was engaged in many different activities throughout his life, including tracking, dog hunting, sandalwood cutting, prospecting, mining, and station work.

His German father, Heinrich (Henry), ran away from an American whaler in 1884 with two companions, Newell and Erickson. These were the days when whaling was done with hand harpoons.

The men had signed their indentures in America. Henry had lived in America with his brother since he was sixteen. After many months at sea, the ship was in port at Albany getting supplies. The ship was about to take the long return trip to America, but the men had no desire to return. It was now or never, so the men tied a change of clothing, food, canvas shoes and a tin of matches in a bundle above their heads and swam the five kilometres to shore. They landed on Middleton Beach.

They were found by Campbell Taylor. He had the Candinup property on the Calgan River and owned Thomas River Station, which is between Esperance and Israelite Bay. Taylor employed them all for four years. All except Newell kept a low profile, as they had a warrant out on them for abandoning ship. Newell returned to Albany before his arrest period of four years had expired, so he had to spend some time in jail.

East West Telegraph Line

Henry Dimer worked for Campbell Taylor for some time, then shepherded for John Paul Brooks at Ballbinia Station. After leaving Ballbinia Station, he bought his own horse team and carted telegraph poles on contract for the first east-west telegraph line. The poles were thrown off Fred Douglas's boat where they floated ashore east of Israelite Bay. Henry Dimer collected the poles from the beach and pulled them up to the top of a hundred-metre cliff. They then carted them one-hundred-and-sixty kilometres to linesmen.

The east-west telegraph line was a significant achievement of the time. It played an important role in the development of Australia, as before it was constructed, communication between Western Australia and the rest of the nation took months (Nullabour Road House). At 4pm on the 8th of December 1877, the first telegraphic message flashed across the Nullarbor. Messages could now be sent and received in a matter of seconds (Monument Australia). Perth was now connected to

Adelaide, via Albany, Esperance, Israelite Bay, Eyre and Eucla and it was an essential part of the overseas communication system.

As the signal was weakened over distance, repeater stations in Western Australia were located at Bremer Bay, Esperance Bay, Israelite Bay, Eyre, Eucla, and in South Australia at Fowlers Bay and Streaky Bay. The hostile conditions of the coast soon played havoc with the reliability of the line. Breakdowns occurred due to corrosion and salt deposits on insulators. When the eastern goldfields were discovered in the early 1890s, Coolgardie became a large telegraph post and the line was extended to the newly discovered goldfields at Norseman (Dundas). The telegraph line was then extended eastwards to Balladonia where a repeater station was constructed and then across country to Eyre. The line was kept inland (following the foot of the escarpment) through to Eucla, thereby withdrawing the path away from the coast and improving reliability (adventures.net.au).

Station Life

After Henry Dimer completed his contract with the east-west telegraph line, he took up a property on top of the cliffs called Whitefoot. This proved a failure, mainly due to his inexperience and the fact that he experienced a very dry first season.

Dimer married Topsie Whitehand ten years after arriving in Australia. They set up their first family home in the settlement at Israelite Bay Telegraph Station. At this time the settlement consisted of the telegraph line repeater station with three operators, two linesmen and a postmaster. The postmaster also taught the local children school lessons. One of the first linesman, John Cook, had twelve children, seven of whom were born at Israelite Bay. The graves of Postmasters John Healey (1898), John Francis (1920), and John Cook (1912) are on the Station (Bickmore).

About 1903, Tom Talbot, George Abbott, and Dimer took up Nanambinia station, which is thirty-two kilometres from Balladonia and one-hundred-and-ninety-two kilometres from Norseman. The station was more than 500,000 acres.

Tom Dimer, the fourth child of Henry and Topsie, was born in a tent that year while their homestead was being built. The first seasons were so dry that Abbott and Talbot left the property, but Dimer and his family remained.

Tom grew up on the station and worked for his father. When he was sixteen, he carried mail and stores from Israelite Bay to Balladonia. The journey took three days.

The Remittance Man

A remittance man was a term for an immigrant from England who was supported by regular payments from their family on the understanding that he would not return home and become a source of embarrassment.

Dimer knew of a remittance man who lived near Baladonia. Once a month he would receive his remittance and then go to Kalgoorlie to socialise at one of the pubs in Hannan Street. Unfortunately, when he was drunk, he did not feel the need for being dressed and would remove his clothes. Although Kalgoorlie was a reasonably tolerant town, this was deemed too much and would put an abrupt end to his partying in Kalgoorlie.

Dinosaur Bones

About 1923, Tom was digging a dam on the property when he unearthed a big hip and other bones of a dinosaur. His sister Bertha took them to Perth to the museum a few months later. The museum identified and kept the bones.

Sandalwood

Tom left the station the following year when he was twenty-one. The station could not support the large family of seven boys and two girls. He worked on properties in South Australia for about a year before returning to Western Australia. He then collected sandalwood around Edjudina with Jack Angel.

Sandalwood is an aromatic wood that has been highly prized for centuries, particularly by the Chinese and Indians. Powdered sandalwood is used in religious ceremonies, and Sandalwood oil is used as a fixative in making soaps and perfumes. Up to the Second World War, before the discovery of penicillin, it was even used to treat venereal disease (Donovan).

Sandalwood is a slow-growing wood with high demand, so it is of high value. In the period of 1844 to 1929, Western Australia was a dominant exporter of sandalwood due to its high quality. It was purchased mainly by Chinese merchants in Singapore and Shanghai to be powdered for incense. By mid-1847, sandalwood mania had gripped the Swan River Colony's population. Some idea of the extent of the boom can be gauged from export figures of the time, which show sandalwood to have risen from virtually zero in 1844 to a position where, in 1848, it challenged whale oil and wool as a leading export earner.

Although the period between 1880 to 1918 was dominated by the discovery of gold in Western Australia, the sandalwood industry also played its part. Sandalwood became known as 'the gold-diggers best friend', as they could rely on its income when gold was scarce (Colbatch). By 1895, alluvial gold in the region was becoming more limited so sandalwood could provide income to enable them to continue prospecting. Between 1896 to 1911 annual export quantities reached 8,000 and 9,000 tonnes. As the price was high, Western Australia exported some 14,355 tons of sandalwood in 1919-1920. Fears that the wood was being overcut resulted in strict new regulations to be introduced in 1923. These regulations were designed to protect the getters, conserve supplies, and ensure that the Crown received due reimbursement for the export of a valuable resource (Satham).

Brumbies

With two helpers Dimer mustered three-hundred wild horses at Yerilla Station (145 kilometres north of Kalgoorlie) and drove them down as far as Grass Patch (seventy-eight kilometres north of Esperance), which is around five-hundred kilometres.

The horses were sold for different purposes, including for meat at a piggery near Kalgoorlie. Tom made enough money to buy a block of land at Circle Valley (approximately twenty kilometres north of Grass Patch).

Wild Dog Hunting

He took one crop off his farm, but the price of dingo and fox heads rose to four dollars, so he decided to sell the farm and become a dogger. He rode from Circle Valley to Nanambinia station, which took him twenty-one days.

Wild dogs often harass, bite and kill sheep, often without eating any. They can also attack and kill smaller cattle. Livestock losses can be high, so control of dingoes and wild dogs occurs in agricultural and pastoral areas to keep numbers down.

Dimer hunted dogs for two years, but the prices dropped, so he then decided to search for Lasseter's lost gold reef in 1931-1932.

Lasseter's Reef

Tom, his brother Wally, Bill Tucker and Fred Whinley, an Aboriginal interpreter, travelled on camels around the Warburton Ranges in search of Lasseter's lost gold reef for four months. They were not the only party that was interested in finding the lost reef around this time. Others, such as Harry Domeyer, John Campbell, the Cables, and Sam Hazlett and his son were also searching for the reef.

In 1929 and 1930, Harold Lasseter claimed he had discovered a rich gold deposit in 1911 or in 1897. On 14 October 1929, he wrote a letter to Kalgoorlie federal member, Albert Green, claiming to have discovered "a vast gold-bearing reef in Central Australia" eighteen years earlier and that it was located at the western edge of the MacDonnell Ranges. No action was taken by the government to investigate the claim. In 1930 he told John Bailey of the Australian Worker's Union that when he was seventeen, he rode from Queensland to the WA Goldfields and discovered a vast gold-bearing reef somewhere near the border of Northern Territory and Western Australia. He claimed that after this discovery he got into difficulties and was rescued by a passing Afghan camel driver who took him to the camp of a surveyor, Joseph Harding. Harding and Lasseter were said to have later returned to the reef in the attempt to fix its location but failed because their watches were inaccurate.

In 1930, Lasseter secured £50,000 from private investors to form an expedition to search for the reef, but it was a complete failure. The lead bushman, Fred Blakeley, believed Lasseter was lying about the Reef. However, the legend of the reef stirred the imagination of adventurous prospectors and the expeditions to find the reef became folklore.

Tom's party set out with nine camels from Rawlinna and headed for the Warburton Range. They took three-hundred pounds of flour, plenty of tea, a seventy-pound bag of sugar and a case of 'tin dog'. Dimer and his party did not carry a large amount of water as they would get it from the local Aboriginals. To do this, they would get up early and look for smoke coming from Aboriginal camps. They would then leave their camels and sit out in the open a few hundred yards away from the Aboriginal camp so they would be seen. The leader of the group would then come out and sit alongside them. Whinley would interpret for the party. Dimer and his party would avoid looking directly at him by sitting side on, as it was disrespectful to look him straight in the eye. In the morning, some women would sometimes come in and stoke up their fire and give them water. Whinley was afraid that the Aboriginals may kill him if he was left alone, so they always stayed vigilant.

At night they would camp with all the camels around them. The camels had bells on them, so if any Aboriginals came nearby, the bell would alert them. If the bells warned them, they would then fire some shots in the air. This was enough to make them run away. Unlike some of the other parties who were searching for the reef, Dimer's party did not have any real conflict with the Aboriginals of the area.

However, like all the other parties searching for the reef, they saw no sign of the fabled reef. All they returned home with was some dog scalps and plenty of stories for the campfire.

Tracker

Dimer had a reputation as an excellent tracker. He learned some tracking skills as a child from Aboriginal children on the station and his own experiences in the bush made him a keen observer.

During the war, he was 'man-powered' and carted ore for the Butterfly mine. One day, the shire secretary, Bill Kerr advised him that a twelve year-old girl, Gwen Rothwell was missing somewhere near Trigg Hill.

He set off in a road board truck with two other men and sat on the bonnet looking for her tracks. Near Mt Norkett, he noticed the girl's tracks and those of a small dog that was thought to be with her. They followed the tracks over Spinifex Hill until they stopped at a dam, where she had a drink of water. Tom noticed that some mud had been disturbed, so he looked around and found further tracks of the girl and the dog.

They lit a fire on Spinifex Hill at sundown and took firesticks for light to follow the tracks. They heard a dog bark and found the girl about twenty-nine kilometres from Trigg Hill.

She said she had become separated from her playmates and thought she was going to spend another night in the bitterly cold bush. Dimer thought having the dog would have given her some warmth the night before, so it was fortunate she had it with her.

Much later, in 1970 when he was spending Easter in Hopetoun with his family on holidays, a police call came over the radio asking for him to report. Two men were lost in the isolated country east of Esperance, and the police party needed his help to track them.

One of the men received news that his father was dying, so they were travelling by car to the Eastern States to arrive there before he died. They were taking a shortcut from Gibson's Soak, but after several miles, the car had broken down about thirty kilometres from Israelite Bay. One of the missing men walked to Israelite Bay for help, and the other man decided to cut through the bush to the east-west road. He soon became lost.

Dimer was able to track the man over the rugged country and over a large escarpment. He could tell from the tracks that the man was in distress due to lack of water. Thirteen days later, the search party found his body. There were only a few hours too late, as he had not been long dead.

Boat Sinking

The following years he had various jobs, one of which he was skipper of a launch for fishing from Esperance. However, this career ended abruptly when the boat sank. The boat was twenty kilometres from shore when the crankshaft broke. The sails had been left on-shore for repair, so Tom made his own sails from the female passengers' coats. The wind took them to the mainland at Stockyard Creek near Rossiter's Bay.

Tom safely landed the passengers onshore in the dinghy. His brother then walked to Esperance to obtain transport for the rest of them. Luckily, all paying customers arrived home safely. Unfortunately for the boat, rough seas came before the launch could be towed to shore and it sank.

Tom Dimer held various jobs in Southern Cross and Kalgoorlie. In 1975 he retired as a Dogger in Kalgoorlie and moved to Perth to retire. He still had some gold in his veins though, as he kept a gold lease in the Leonora area with two partners.

Chapter Fourteen

Merton and Mertondale

IN THE LATE 1800'S, AS NEW GOLD STRIKES were made, towns were springing up like mushrooms all over the goldfields. One such town was Mertondale which was thirty kilometres north-east of Leonora. The man who first discovered gold there was Fred Merton. Like many other men of this era, his story became legendary.

Merton has become a character full of myth, legend and contradiction. Over time there have been conflicting accounts of Merton's personality, the facts relating to his gold discovery and his management of the mine. This makes it hard to distinguish fact from fiction.

Merton was an enthusiastic prospector, and he prospected in areas close to existing finds. His talent was to spot what others had missed. He also had the tenacity to develop his discovery into a solely owned and managed mine. He was initially instrumental in establishing several gold mines around Broad Arrow before turning his attention to the area around Mt Malcolm. Apparently, Fred Merton and his party had been so successful at the Australian Peer mine that Merton used a 30cm-square slab of stone, studded with coarse gold, as a paperweight.

Eventually, the gold gave out, and there are differing accounts of what happened next. The differing accounts arose because his former colleague made a claim against Merton's new find. This colleague was William Callagher and he argued in Court that they were partners and he was entitled to a half share of the mine. Merton denied this, and the Supreme Court eventually found in his favour.

Later reports on the find usually state that Merton and his mate, William Callagher (sometimes spelt Gallagher), decided to go prospecting and they had a gentleman's agreement to share anything found. In March 1899, while Merton was looking for a lost horse before moving camp, he noticed a stony ridge that looked promising. The ridge was on the way from Cue to Mount Margaret and thirteen kilometres north of the Australian Peer mine. He examined the outcrop and to his delight found the quartz to be speckled with gold. It was one of the richest quartz reefs he had ever seen. He immediately pegged out a reward claim and a ten-hectare block. He lodged his claims at the registrar's office, which were granted.

Callagher claimed in the subsequent court case that Merton found the gold while looking for a horse. The next day, which was a Sunday, he went to the area on his bicycle and pegged the claim. On Monday he told Callagher he was going into town to buy food and did not advise

Callagher of the find ("Important Mining Action – Callagher v Merton", *The West Australian*, [Perth, 14 September 1899, p7).

Another person who knew both men claimed that Merton offered a half share to Callagher, who laughed it off, not believing it. When Callagher went to the new mine, Merton told him it was too late to claim his share.

These accounts implied that Merton deliberately set out to swindle his mate.

Merton never claimed to be a mate or partner of Callagher. Evidence suggests that he indeed had no partnership arrangement with Callagher, as at the time of pegging out the leases he was short of funds and 'would have taken twenty pounds from anyone to go in with him in his new venture', but no one would. The blacksmith, Jack Cotter, loaned him ten pounds and the Malcolm store, run by the Johnson Brothers, allowed him credit. This enabled Merton to retain full ownership of the leases. ("Merton's Reward", *Coolgardie Miner*, 12 May 1899, p6)

Some later accounts of the story also stated that Callagher lodged an objection on the leases claiming they were 'mates and should share the bonanza' and the Warden found for Merton, claiming the partnership had been dissolved before Merton applied for his lease. Research by Chappell disputes this. No newspaper reports of the time ever mentioned a partner, and there were never reports of any proceedings in the Warden's court. In the Supreme Court case, no mention was made of any hearing in the Warden's Court. Callagher did file a caveat over the leases with the Mining Registrar to protect his punitive half interest, so James J Robinson was appointed joint manager with Merton for the first year of operations (Chappell 24).

Merton's account of events, which he presented to the Supreme Court disputes Callagher's version that they had a verbal partnership agreement. Merton claimed that 'we were not in any manner whatever concerned as mates and are not now interested in any other properties as mates or partners'.

He claimed that Callagher received a one-quarter share in the Deerah lease plus food in return for labour and there was never any verbal agreement to become mates or partners in equal shares on new discoveries. Merton also employed others on the mine so that he could prospect when he wanted. This arrangement continued for fourteen months. This arrangement was profitable for Callagher, as Merton paid for all the expenses.

In his evidence and in newspaper interviews, he makes no mention of searching for horses and states that Callagher only became interested in the lease after his third crushing. At this time, Merton claims that Callagher asked him for a one-quarter interest in the mine and when Merton refused he replied: "if I don't get a cut I'll cause you trouble".

Callagher filed a case at the Supreme Court and won, despite his self-contradictory evidence. Chappell suggests that this verdict demonstrated the power of the 'cheated mate' myth on the jury.

A notice of appeal was given, and by December of that year, Merton won the Full Court decision against Callagher. The three judges were unanimous in the decision that the finding of the jury should be set aside and a verdict 'exactly the opposite of that of the jury' should be returned. Callagher was granted leave to appeal to the Privy Council, but he failed to do so within the required three-month period.

On 20 March 1900, Chief Justice Onslow discharged the Receiver Manager and dissolved the injunction restraining Merton from accessing half the proceeds of gold won from the Merton's Reward property. He also ordered the removal of all the caveats which Callagher had lodged against Merton's leases (Chappell 34).

Callagher may have lost the final court case, but Merton's reputation was damaged. The myth of the cheating partner instigated by Callagher was perpetuated, partly due to the reporting of the case at the time. Callagher's version of events presented in court was printed, and Merton's account was largely edited.

Early recollections of the court case did not dispute the findings. However, in 1945 Charles Harris claimed they were partners and Merton engineered a split in the partnership so that he could claim the full reward for the find (Harris 23). He blended fact with fiction and his version of events that Merton was a rogue who manipulated his mate out of a fortune set the tone for future accounts of the tale (Chappell 39). Based on Chappell's research, the finding of the Supreme Court, and the early reporting on the find, I believe that Merton did not swindle his 'mate'. As one digger commented, it is amazing how many mates you have after you find gold!

Returning to the early history of the mine, Merton at first employed two men to bag the rich stone and he carted it to the Waitekauri battery for crushing. There are conflicting reports as to how much ore and gold Merton produced in the first few months, some were highly exaggerated. According to Chappell, by the end of 1899 Merton had won 3,306.75 ounces gold gross weight which, even at a conservative £3/15s per ounce, would have been worth £12,400. The news of his good results bought in a rush of other miners to the area, who began prospecting and pegging in the area ("Merton's Reward – F Merton Interviewed", *Coolgardie Miner,* 7 June 1899, p6) (P.W.H. Theil & Co 252).

Not only prospectors rushed to the area. Merton's younger brother Frank also turned up at the mine, demanding a share of the mine. A witness heard Fred reply, "Take your coat off and work like your brother Herb, and I will pay you good wages". When Fred refused his request, Frank produced a gun. Fred ran to his house where both brothers fired shots at each other 'in a brotherly fashion'. It was reported that Fred finally agreed to pay for a one-way passage to South Africa where a four-figure sum of money would be waiting for him. (Chappell 20). However, a former employee later wrote that this event became distorted in the newspapers over time and that Frank did not go to South Africa until 1892. If Fred did give him money, it seems that his brother Frank was far more successful at extracting a share of the profits that Callagher was.

Frank had recently been acquitted over the fatal shooting of an Afghan camel-driver during a failed expedition from Coolgardie to South Australia. The expedition lost nine camels from thirst. Evidence was given that the Afghan was crazed from thirst and attacked another member of the party. Frank shot the Afghan to save him (*Coolgardie Miner,* 13 November 1952, p4).

Reproduction of an image contained in "Merton's Reward Claim", *The North Queensland Register*, 11 November 1901, p25

Before long, a suitable site for a town was selected on a flat plain near the mine. Streets were marked out, and the blocks pegged. Warden Burt said he would wait a while before issuing business licences, as it was 'a great expense to the government indiscriminately establishing towns all over the goldfields'. He also delayed granting hotel licences, as he wanted 'to see leases developed, not men made drunk'.

In May it was discovered that a new line of reef appeared to run through the camping ground. This caused new leases to be pegged, several of them by the Governor's aide-de-camp. By June there were one-hundred men in the area, with the mine buildings and battery under construction. In early July a coach service started, running three times a week between Leonora and Merton's Reward, as it was then called. At the end of the month, Cobb & Co began a daily service.

At the new townsite, fifty-two blocks were sold on Saturday 19 August 1899. Prices ranged from £20 to £210 for a block bought by Merton. Sixty-three blocks were soon sold for an average of £54 7s 3d. A Progress Committee was formed, and sites were chosen for a hospital, cemetery, sanitary depot, and recreation reserves. The Government agreed to sink a well to provide a water supply. Building begun almost immediately, starting with two stores and a hotel (Warden Burt must have relented!).

While all this activity was occurring, the mine produced sensational values from the fabulously rich pocket. Merton took the bold step to operate the mine himself. By December 1899 he employed forty-six men to mine the ore. Merton was joint mine manager with Robinson, assayer, gold escort, engineer and accountant.

Future mine owners claimed his mining method was haphazard and they found vast unsupported caverns underground. However, in her thesis, Chappell argues that he "followed locally accepted mining practice. He understood the limitations of his style of management and sold when changing conditions within the mine threatened to surpass them". She also noted that "Despite its appearance, however, it was apparently a safe mine. There were no reports of death or serious injury under Merton's management" (Chappell 111).

Merton was able to develop the mine without external finance due to the favourable geology. "A freakish combination of orebody geometry and topography combined to produce extensive outcrops of rubble-like gold-bearing quartz which could be raked up, bagged and sent to a stamp battery. The mine paid for itself from the outset" (Chappell 11).

He erected a ten-head mill (that increased to thirty-head by the time of its sale), power units and batteries of Babcock's boilers. Many thought he was over-optimistic to invest so much, but by the end of September 1901 it had produced £76,500 worth of gold. The gamble of erecting his own battery paid off (Chappell 58).

His mining and milling costs were low, despite paying higher wages than any other mine in the field. The following was later written about how the mine was worked before flotation as a company:

> The mine was both easily and cheaply worked. In fact, though it seems incredible, two men mining in the bottom open cut were able to keep the 20 stamps going 16 hours a day. The method of breaking down was a simple one. Each man 'jumped' a hole down to a depth of about twelve foot. The hole was then charged and fired, with the result that from thirty to forty tons of milling ore was broken out. By this simple means, the men found no difficulty in keeping the battery going. Big as the mine was, it employed

only about thirty men all told. Mr Merton was his own mine and mill manager and combined the two positions with great profit to himself. The mining was done cheaply, and the milling results were all that could be desired, a high extraction being secured, and the gold being of good average value (Harris H, "The Northern Fields – Merton's Reward: Early Years", *Kalgoorlie Miner,* 3 March 1936, p3).

There are two schools of thought about Merton, both vastly different. One is that 'Miser' Merton had gone insane with success, and he was a controlling gun-toting miser with some unusual hobbies. One slanderous report states: "His suspicions almost amounted to insanity and his meanness was beyond the contempt of a miser. The place on top of the hill where he housed his miserable self is said to be riddled with bullets which he nightly fired at imaginary burglars" ("Miser Merton – Caught by Kaufman – The Morals of Mateship". *West Australian Sunday Times,* [Perth] 9 February 1902, p10). He played with gold, made statuettes of himself, men and horses from it while waiting for the crushing to take place. A photo of him next of a large pile of gold and a carved statue was widely circulated. It was also reported that he carelessly spilt gold as if it were worthless, which only a crazy person would do.

There was also a report that when Merton went on a trip some workers were thrown off the mine and had to fend for themselves. However, an employee later stated that some men were run out of town. This was because they put all their costs from a night out at a shanty on the slate under Frank's brother Herb's name. The Shanty was run by Bill Harvey and his wife. The wife was away for the evening, and her husband was illiterate, so he was unaware that one of the few nondrinkers of the town was being charged for all the drinks.

The other view of Merton is that he was a kind generous man with random acts of philanthropy.

An ex-employee years later stated that he paid good wages and was the best boss he had ever had. He would pay a full day's wage for any small job. He also wrote that although Merton could not give jobs to everyone who asked, he often wrote cheques to men carrying swags looking for employment (McDonald D. S., "Mertons and Mertondale", *Coolgardie Miner*, 13 November 1952, p4). He certainly seemed to polarise opinion.

It was rumoured that Merton deliberately set out to give the impression that he had so much gold that he could play with it to attract an unwary buyer. The Kauffman's Group in London bought the mine through their Kalgoorlie representative, Bewick, Moreing and Co. The purchase price was not disclosed although £100,000 with shares was rumoured, it may have been as low as £10,000 with shares. *The Malcolm Chronicle* commented that: 'It is just about as difficult to ascertain the amount which changed hands as it was to ascertain the actual monthly output of gold from Merton's battery'. Chappell believes that it was most likely a cash component of between £10,000 and £40,000 plus £70,000 in fully paid shares, which would have provided him with up to £80,000 in the bank for himself and his family (Chappell 67-71). Research into the sale of the mine has concluded that the sale price was artificially inflated to make the mine appear more valuable (Chappell 6).

Merton was indeed a shrewd operator, as he had taken the best of the gold and knew his limitations. He timed the sale of his mine perfectly. There is no evidence to suggest that he was not sane. Indeed, his actions suggest the opposite. He left the mine while it was still profitable, he had excellent production records and operated the mine with low working costs. Albert Gaston wrote that Merton had 'the best one-man show in Australia'. As there were few, if any one-man operations of the size of Merton's Reward, this claim could indeed be true (Chappell 118).

At the end of January 1902, Fred Morgan assumed control of the mine on behalf of Merton's Reward Gold Mining Company Ltd. The mine now belonged to a typical British mining company. They invested heavily, and the oxidised ore did not last long, and they ran into sulphides. They also had a high turnover of mine managers, five within six years. This made it difficult for them to come to a crucial understanding of the mine's geology.

Among the managers were Messrs Huntley, Young, Morgan and Wheatley. Huntley put in a cyanide plant to treat the sands left after the battery had finished crushing the stones. These had high values, so the reports going back to England did not show a loss at this stage. G F Young worked under Huntley for a few months before taking over the managership. His job was to get the plant operating again. He disconnected twenty stamps, leaving only ten in the battery. When Young became the mine manager, he installed a filter press, which brought good returns. He also cleaned up the rubbish around and under the floors of the battery where Merton had allegedly been careless with the amalgam. This brought in another 6,220 grams of gold.

Early one evening, an explosion was heard from the surface of the mine. Smoke billowed from the building that was used as a storeroom. Inside this storeroom was a vault with a two-tonne Chub door. It was presumed by those who heard the explosion that this had been blown up by thieves.

After much discussion among the crowd that had gathered at the scene, Young ordered a carpenter to take a couple of sheets of iron off the roof so that lanterns might be lowered into the office to reveal the thieves who were thought to be still there. By this time, the men working the mine had been brought up to the surface and were armed with lanterns and weapons. They formed a strong cordon around the building. The lanterns were duly lowered into the office, but no one was to be seen.

The nearest policeman was fifty kilometres away in Leonora, so the manager thought it was his duty to investigate the storeroom. He was accompanied by the accountant, both with revolvers in hand. The miners crept closer to the building and one mistook a shadow for a burglar and fired his gun. The bullet went through the office desk and out the galvanised-iron roof, narrowly missing the manager and accountant.

Pandemonium broke loose. The men rushed in to catch the thieves, but none were to be found within the office. The burglars had plugged the keyholes of the safe with dynamite, inserted a detonator and long fuse, then lit the fuse. They hid a safe distance away and after the explosion came back to find that the heavy iron door was only cracked. However, if they did manage to open the vault, they would only have found forty pounds worth of gold! It was rumoured that the attempted robbery was the work of Jim Mahoney's gang. Mahoney was later shot at Leonora while trying to steal gold from a mine.

The mine that was once hailed as a second Kalgoorlie operated for only five more years. By 1910, apart from the low-grade ore in the sulphides, all the gold had been processed. After the mine closed, the gold mining leases were transferred to Charles Kaufman, who held them until his death.

As for Merton, he had a second successful career over-east and became one of the 'best known racing men in Australia'. He won the Caulfield cup in 1910 with Flavinius and again in 1913 with Aurifier.

He paid his jockey, W H Smith a retainer of five-hundred pounds per year and ten-percent of any first, second or third stake money his mounts won. Mr Smith was recognised as one of the best jockeys in the Commonwealth. Smith's income from the Merton Stable alone in 1912 "would make the mouth of most punters water".

He had good horses and good riders and was often first in important races. Smith was killed riding one of his horses in March 1914. Merton believed Smith was infallible and incorruptible and Merton resolved to have nothing more to do with racing after his favourite jockey's death, except as an intermittent punter ("Idolised His Jockey – Mr Fred Merton", *The Herald,* [Melbourne], 1 November 1923, p3).

Fred Merton. Reference Image from *The Herald*, [Melbourne], 1 November 1923, p3

He was also renowned for throwing handfuls of pennies from his motor car in the poorer parts of Sydney for the children. 'This giving of money to the poor and wresting it from the bookmakers are his two hobbies, and he indulges freely in both." ("Merton and His Jockey" *The Cumberland Argus and Fruitgrowers Advocate* [Parramatta] 5 November 1913, p2).

The Daily News reported in October 1949 that he was to fly for the first time from Sydney to attend his forty-sixth Melbourne Cup at eighty-two years of age. They also reported that he painted doll faces for the local children's hospital in his spare time ("He's Making His First Air Trip to His 46th Cup" *The Daily News* [Perth], 28 October 1949, p1).

Merton the Miser or Merton the Philanthropist? I will let you decide.

As for the town, within a few years after the mine's closure, little remained. There was the main shaft, the cement foundations, some rusting boilers at the mine site, a crumbling wall of one of the four hotels, a few heaps of rubbish half hidden in the bush, and some sand and slime dumps.

My great-grandfather, Harry Dower, brought his family out to the old ghost-town of Mertondale during 1935. He set up a cyanide treatment plant to process the old residues from the mine, and they lived here for approximately a year.

He wrote to the Education Department and arranged correspondence lessons for my Nanna, Norma and her sister Vera.

The house Harry made was very makeshift. Norma claimed, 'my father could not have been described as a handyman by any feat of the imagination'. Two bedrooms were built by weighing down sheets of corrugated-iron across two of the long, thick cement foundations. He reasoned these would serve instead of walls. Each end was filled in, a divider put in the room and two doors installed. Their summer-room kitchen was a thatched bough-shed with a tent nearby if the weather proved too unkind for eating under the flimsy shelter.

To her dismay, my Great Grandmother Kate had to cook outside on iron bars over an open fireplace, and she had a camp oven for baking. After a few 'burnt offerings', she became quite proficient in this style of cooking. In time she proudly produced light sponge cakes from the formerly despised camp oven.

They drew their water supply from a well nearly two kilometres from their home. Norma helped her father with this chore by turning one handle of the windlass as they pulled bucket after bucket from the well. One day a snake came up in a bucket of water. My Nanna had to hold the handle steady while he tipped the bucket over and killed the snake.

Norma and Vera found plenty to keep themselves occupied with when they finished their school-work for the day. Their home was among the old mine workings and close to where the gold had been smelted from the mine. They soon learned that if they paned off the dirt in this area, they could always find a trace of gold in the panning-off dish. Their father taught them how to pan-off correctly, and they saved the specs of gold in 'poverty pots'.

They spent much time exploring the district and scavenging eagerly among the old rubbish dumps, many of which were overgrown with bushes. They found oddly shaped purple bottles and porcelain jars with the labels still clearly lettered. If only they realised the value these articles would have in later years!

Although they had few visitors and life was generally uneventful, there were a few memorable incidents that broke the monotony. The "Mystery of the Light' caught their imagination as children. Harry was pumping the cyanide solution into the vats of sand as part of the process of extracting gold one still, moonlit evening. He noticed a light in the bush to the east. It seemed too bright to be the reflection of the moon on broken glass or tin. He called the rest of the family, and they decided the light must be from someone's camp. They drove toward the light to offer hospitality to the stranger. They were puzzled to find that the closer they got to the light, the further away it seemed to be. Finally, it disappeared altogether. They saw this light on other occasions but never discovered the source. He told his daughters that is was probably a 'Min Min' light or 'will-o'-the-wisp' that Aboriginal people and bushmen often spoke of.

Another exciting event was the night of the big storm. One summer night a violent storm swept through the old mine workings, making the air chokingly thick with dust swept up from the sand and slime dumps. As the insecure roof on the bedrooms began lifting and falling alarmingly, Harry climbed onto the roof to add more weights. Norma wanted to help but was sternly told to stay inside, where she was safe from flying sheets of iron. The roof stayed on, but after the storm had subsided they saw that most of the thatching on the bough-shed had blown away and the tent had collapsed. There was a lot of rebuilding and cleaning to be done the next day.

Not long after the storm, my Great-grandfather decided that the treatment plant was no longer a paying proposition (or perhaps my Great-grandmother had finally had enough?), so they packed up and left their ghost-town. With their departure, Mertondale settled back once again into slumber.

Chapter Fifteen

When Nobody Cared

My purse and my body were lean.
My clothes weren't fit to be seen.
I was always alone, with never a chum.
I haunted the hills with my trusty old 'brum'.
A 'cussing the strike that refused to be struck,
And 'cussing creation along 'me luck.
A lonely, unknown, insignificant man.
A 'mixin my dough in a rusty old pan.
 - And nobody cared.

Came days when I surely was blue.
Tobacco smoked sticky as glue.
The brumby shed tears every time that he brayed.
And got on my nerves till they quivered and frayed.
The sky was a drizzle, the bushes were wet.
The fire wouldn't burn, and the billy upset.
The damper was doughy, the bully was tough.
And God only knows how I swallowed the stuff.

When Nobody Cared

The goanna was putrid, the gnamma hole stank.
And the quandong conserve was bitter and rank.
But I never abated a lick.
Of that battered old shovel and pick,
And still in my battered old tambrey I dreamed
Of the strike overhead, till my features grey seamed,
And my fingers grew knotted, and over my head,
The silver of age was beginning to spread.
And my breeches were torn, in a way that still brings
The hot blush of shame when I think of. these things
- And nobody cared.

And then I uncovered the lode.
That's where I resigned from the road.
It was rich as Scotch salmon, ten ounces or so.
Now the people say 'Mister' wherever I go.
And they wag their glad tails, and roll over for me.
If I give them a smile they're as pleased as can be;
For that lick of the pick made a different man.
From the one who mixed dough in his rusty old pan.
- When nobody cared.

The above poem was written by Roddy McLeod. Roddy was a Scotsman who travelled extensively in North and South America and South Africa, before coming to Australia. When gold was found at Coolgardie, he went overland from Queensland with two pack horses. He prospected on the way and struck the Coolgardie road at Yellowdine in March 1898.

He prospected every new find on the field and discovered country from Norseman to Nullagine. Twice he nearly perished, once near Lake Lefroy and again at Lake Way.

Roddy was shot in the shoulder by an Afghan, and on another occasion, he was rescued from his blazing camp after being severely burned.

He was always alone, never prospected with a mate. In his swag, he had copies of classics and Oman Khayyam. Oman Khayyam was a Persian mathematician, astronomer, and poet.

He lived the last of his days in Upper Swan with his sister (*Daily News* [Perth], 25 August 1934, p19).

People Mentioned

Aarons, G, 147

Abbott, George, 164

Alderdice, J G, 122

Angel, Jack, 165

Ashwin, Arthur, 82

Bailey, George, 6

Bailey, John, 168

Balzano, James, 117

Bamlett, Joe, 94

Bamlett, Joe C H, 94

Bathe, W, 55

Beale, M, 83

Bennetts, George, 136

Billy the Fowl, 157

Bissenberger, 48

Black Christie, 85

Black, R S, 147

Blakeley, Fred, 168

Bower, Tom, 114

Bowler, W, 44

Breen, Mick, 44

Brogan, Billy, 32

Brooks, John Paul, 162

Brown, Clarrie, 81

Brown, Dr G Havard, 62

Cable, Jim, 73

Callaghan, Constable, 20

Callagher, William, 173

Campell, John, 167

Carnegie, David, 11

Carter, Peter, 7, 8, 141

Charlie the Goose, 78

Climie, 154

Connors, Tom, 32

Cook, John, 164

Cook, Sam, 32

Cotter, Jack, 174

Cotter, W J, 122

Cottingham, 48

Cutbush, Host, 61

Dawson, Henry, 141

De Baun, John, 55

People Mentioned

Dempsey, Jack, 23
d'Everylns, Duncan, 125
Devine, Ainslea, 89
Dimer, Heinrich (Henry), 161
DIMER, TOM, 161
Dimer, Topsie, 163
Domeyer, Harry, 167
Dooley, Mick, 107
Douglas, Fred, 162
Douglas, Lord Percy, 47
Dower, Henry Joseph, 133
Dower, Joseph Henry (Harry), 187
Dower, Kate (nee Hancock), 188
Doyle, Jack, 131, 137
Doyle, Tom, 58, 59, 138
Dr Gibson, 121
Duff, Tom, 147
Duggan, Constable, 127
Dunn, John George, 151
Dunn, Wilson, 61
Elliott, Thomas, 141, 146
Ewing, Dr, 62
Fingall, Lord, 145, 154, 155

Finnerty, Warden, 7, 38
Forrest, Alexander, 152
Forrest, Sir John, 107
Francis, John, 164
Frost, Billy, 76
Galthrop, H, 71
Gardiner, William, 141
Gaston, Albert, 183
German Charlie, 48
Gibb, William, 119
Green, Albert, 168
Greeson, Arthur, 56
Gwynne, R, 44
Hales, Smiler, 103
Hamblin, W J, 75
Hamblin, Walter, 97
Harding, Joseph, 168
Harkness, Thomas, 54
Harris, Charles, 176
Hassell, A. W., 152
Hazlett, Sam, 167
Healey, John, 164
Heppingstone, John, 45
Hilder, Jim, 45

People Mentioned

Hillier-Lacye, 93

Holland, Dr, 63

Huxley, John, 141

Island, Charlie, 157

Jackson, Harold, 127

Jacky (Tracker), 128

Jacobs, Tassie, 137

James, John, 65

Jerger, H, 61

Johnston, J, 55

Kaufman, Charles, 185

Kay, Jim, 12

Kerr, Bill, 169

Kerr, Billy, 32

Kiernan, Jack, 13

King, Norma (nee Dower), 187

Larkings, Percy, 46

Larkins, Percy, 45

Lasseter, Harold, 168

Liex, Bernie, 80

Lightly, District Mine Inspector, 122

Lindsay, David, 154

Lindsay, W H, 146

Long Charlie, 53

Long Tom, 63

Long, Father, 17, 18

Love, Tom, 155

Lowry, Henry, 22

Mahoney, Jim, 185

Maori Bill, 48

Marmion, W. E., 152

Marshall, John, 28

Maskell, F E, 93

Matthews, Joe, 32

McAdam, Frank, 119

McAuliffe, Jerry, 43

McCleod, May, 62

McDonald, D. S., 182

McGauchy, William, 119

McGennett, 73

McGorkill, Wallace, 118

McGrath, Ted, 46

McGregor, Jas F, 134

McKenzie, 'Camel', 154

McLeod, Roddy, 192

McManus, F J, 48

McNeil, Neil, 152

People Mentioned

Mentor, Billy, 114

Merton, Frank, 177

Merton, Fred, 172

Metzke Bros, 83

Micklejohn, 38, 48

Miller, Don, 35

Mills, John, 7, 141

Milson, Charles, 119

Monger and Co., 152

Monkey, 45

Moondyne Joe, 77

Morton, Joe, 11

Murphy, John, 119, 121

Murray, Jack, 35

North, Colonel, 150

O'Callaghan, Dennis (Dinny), 1

O'Connor, Tassie, 19, 59

O'Connor, Tassy, 58

O'Callaghan, Dennis, 144

O'Callaghan, Dinny, 117

O'Connor, Tassy, 45, 47

O'Grady, Hubert, 81

Onslow, Chief Justice, 176

Palmer, Joe, 68

Pearce, Sam, 93

Pearce, W, 83

Pearson, Charles, 22

Pellew, J H, 134

Pickering, Jack, 73

Piesse, F H, 132

Quigley, Victoria, 126

Quinn, Margaret, 125

Reason, Henry, 81

Reynolds, Billy, 9

Reynolds, W J, 134

Robinson, James Johnson, 175

Rope, Jim, 27

Rothwell, Gwen, 169

Rutland, Vera (nee Dower), 187

Samuels, Jack, 46

Shaw, J, 145

Shaw, Jim, 7

Shriven, Otto, 48

Simm, George, 56

Simon, J L, 83

Smith, Bryan, 138

Smith, Sergeant, 60

Sudely, Lord, 154

PEOPLE MENTIONED

Tait, A L, 62
Talbot, Tom, 164
Taylor, Campbell, 162
The Yank, 78
Tierney, Jack, 154
Tindale, Engineer, 134
Trotter, Job, 49
Tucker, Bill, 167
Tulloch, Jack, 81
Vinden, George, 92
Vivienne, May, 59
Watt, Harry, 56
Watty, Bill, 147
Weston, Bill, 35

Wheeler, Mike, 138
Whinley, Fred, 167
Whitehand, Topsie, 163
Wickercraft, John, 121
Williams, Billie, 13
Willis, Jim, 81
Wilson, Ken, 119
Wittenoom, F, 132
Wyatt, Billy, 65
Wyatt, James, 65
Wyrill, Rev A, 62
Yank, 157
Young, G F, 183

Works Cited

"A history of sandalwood cutting in Western Australia." Perth: Unpublished typescript of interview held by Battye Library, 1975. Transcript.

adventures.net.au. *Telegraph Line*. 2018. <http://www.adventures.net.au/information/telegraph-track/>.

Bell Sally and Eaton, Caitlin. *Gold Fields in the goldfields, a short history of gold fields in Australia*. Ed. Sally Bell. Gold Fields Ltd. West Perth, n.d. PDF. <https://www.goldfields.com/pdf/about-us/about-gold-fields/gold-fields-in-australia/gf-in-australia.pdf>.

Bickmore, Jill. *Australian Cemeteries*. 2004. <http://www.australiancemeteries.com.au/wa/esperance/esperancelonedata.htm>.

Bough, Robert. *Wealth for the Willing: The Story of Kanowna*. Victoria Park: Bough, R, 2016.

Chappell, M D P. *Merton's Reward Gold Mine: Reconstructing the mine and deconstructing the myth*. Perth: Murdoch University, 2013. <http://researchrepository.murdoch.edu.au/id/eprint/20220/2/02Whole.pdf>.

WORKS CITED

Colbatch, H. *Story of One Hundred Years*. Perth: Government Printer, 1926.

Compton, G and Manners, R. "The Early History of Kalgoorlie's Goldrushes." Perth, 1993.

Golden Mile Loopline Railway Society. *About Our Train*. n.d. 2018. <http://www.loopline.com.au/Loopline/About-our-Train/>.

Harris, C M. "The Margaret and the Murchison Fields." *Early Days – Journal and Proceedings of the WA Historical Society* 3.7 (1945): 23.

Kimberley, Warren Bert. "History of Western Australia: A narrative of her past together with biographies of her leading men." Melbourne: F. W. Niven & Co, 1897.

King, Norma. "First Kanowna Bank was a Tent." *Kalgoorlie Miner*, 3 February 1979.

Monument Australia. *East-West Telegraph Line*. 2018, 2 October 2018. <http://monumentaustralia.org.au/themes/technology/industry/display/60459-east-west-telegraph-line>.

Nullabour Road House. *Remnants of a Lost Town: The Eucla Telegraph Station*. 24 09 2015. <https://www.nullarborroadhouse.com.au/remnants-of-a-lost-town-the-eucla-telegraph-station/>.

O'Callaghan, Denis. *Long Life Reminiscences and Adventures Throughout the World*. Perth, 1941.

P.W.H. Theil & Co. *Twentieth century impressions of Western Australia*. Perth: P.W.H. Theil & Co, 1901.

Red5 Limited. "Darlot Gold Mine." 2016. *red5limited.com*. 2018. <http://red5limited.com/darlot/>.

Satham, Pamela. "The Sandalwood Industry in Australia: A History - WA Sandalwood Nuts." 1990. <http://www.wasandalwoodnuts.com.au/js/tiny_mce/plugins/filem

anager/files/The_Sandalwood_Industry_in_Australia_-_A_History.pdf>.

Sharp, Moya. "Darlot - Ghost Town." 14 August 2017. *Outback Family History Blog.* Blog. 2018. <https://www.outbackfamilyhistoryblog.com/2017/08/14/darlot-ghost-town/>.

Sheriff", "The 1896 Coolgardie WA Cycle Express Company" *Local Post.* 28 May 2010. <https://www.stampboards.com/viewtopic.php?f=23&t=11285>.

Printed in Great Britain
by Amazon